SECRET PLACES
of
Staten Island

A Visitor's Guide to Scenic
and Historic Treasures of Staten Island

PROTECTORS
OF PINE OAK
WOODS

STATEN ISLAND'S
LAND CONSERVATION
ORGANIZATION

Bruce Kershner

Sponsored by
Protectors of
Pine Oak Woods, Inc.

KENDALL/HUNT PUBLISHING COMPANY
4050 Westmark Drive   Dubuque, Iowa 52002

All photographs and panorama illustrations by Bruce Kershner, unless noted otherwise below.

Generous permission was given to use the following graphics:

Cover photos: Snowy Egret by Harry Madden
(from upper right clockwise)   Spring Pond by Mike Feller © 1998
                                       Beach and Waterfall scenes by
                                           John and Margie Prasek.

Illustrations by Olive Earle from *Staten Island Walk Book* (1962),
    Jasper Cropsey painting (page x) and photos on pages 65 (right)
    and 128: S.I. Institute of Arts & Sciences

Naturalist photos on page 15 and historical illustrations on page 92
    used with permission of S.I. Historical Society

Spring Pong photo (page 136): Mike Feller, copyright © 1998

Photos by John and Margie Prasek, Harry Madden, Joni Note, James Rossi, Herman Zaage, Jim Scarcella and Scotty Jenkins are credited where appropriate.

The authors assume no personal responsibility for any actions, or results of these actions, of the reader in choosing to visit the features described in this book.

To order a copy of this book directly from the publisher, call 1-800-228-0810.

Secret Places of Staten Island
TABLE OF CONTENTS

Staten Island Road Map

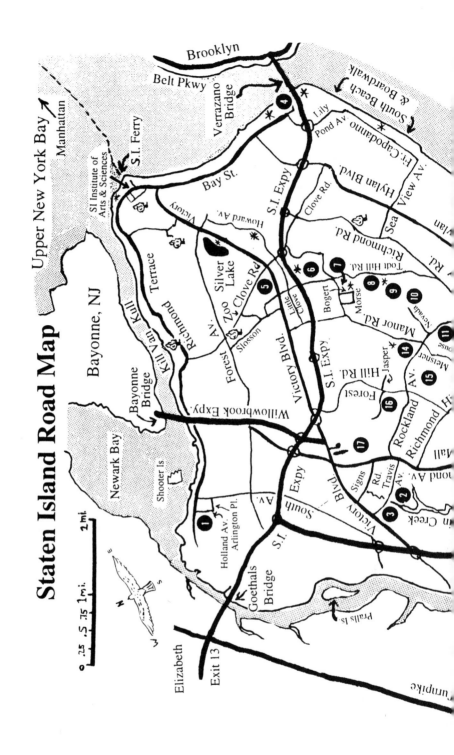

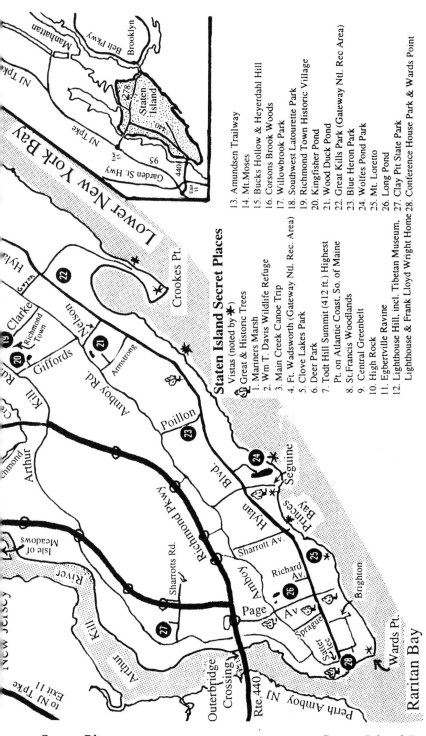

Staten Island Secret Places

Vistas (noted by ★)
✿ Great & Historic Trees
1. Mariners Marsh
2. Wm T. Davis Wildlife Refuge
3. Main Creek Canoe Trip
4. Ft. Wadsworth (Gateway Ntl. Rec. Area)
5. Clove Lakes Park
6. Deer Park
7. Todt Hill Summit (412 ft.) Highest
   Pt. on Atlantic Coast, So. of Maine
8. St.Francis Woodlands
9. Central Greenbelt
10. High Rock
11. Egbertville Ravine
12. Lighthouse Hill, incl. Tibetan Museum,
    Lighthouse & Frank Lloyd Wright Home

13. Amundsen Trailway
14. Mt.Moses
15. Bucks Hollow & Heyerdahl Hill
16. Corsons Brook Woods
17. Willowbrook Park
18. Southwest Latourette Park
19. Richmond Town Historic Village
20. Kingfisher Pond
21. Wood Duck Pond
22. Great Kills Park (Gateway Ntl. Rec Area)
23. Blue Heron Park
24. Wolfes Pond Park
25. Mt. Loretto
26. Long Pond
27. Clay Pit State Park
28. Conference House Park & Wards Point

Secret Places   v   *Staten Island Road Map*

ACKNOWLEDGMENTS

Producing this book was truly a teamwork effort. Without the help of the following people, this historic book would not have been possible. A debt of gratitude goes to those who helped me edit and proof the manuscript: Sylvia Zaage, Joni Note, John Rooney, Jim Rossi, Cap Field, Mike Feller, and Ed Johnson. Thank you for providing me with food and hospitality during my field work: Sylvia Breitberg, Toni Buegler, and my mom, Pearl Kershner.

Thanks so much for your effort and great generosity in contributing photos: Joni Note, John Prasek, Harry Madden, Jim Rossi, Mike Feller, Jack Baird, Herman Zaage, Jim Scarcella, Scotty Jenkins and S.I. Institute. Thank you, my daughter Libby, for being my trail companion and secretary.

For those who walked me through the trails and/or the text, thanks from the bottom of my heart: Cap Field, John Rooney, Tim Williams, Steve Pichler, Jack and Lois Baird, George Pratt, Herman Zaage, Elsa Haas, Jim Scarcella, Karl Alderson, Dominick Durso, Hillel Lofaso, Bonnie Petite, Howard Snyder and Catherine Barron, Richard Lynch, Carlton Beil, Mike Arale, Dr. Stephen Clements; Ed Johnson, Ray Matarazzo and Ed Gregory (S.I. Institute of Arts & Sciences); Mary Gibson Scott, Bill Tate, Martin O'Toole (Gateway N.R.A.); Kathie Nutt and Stephanie Bonaguera (Greenbelt Park); Dorothy Reilly (Tibetan Museum); William McMillan and Carlotta Defillo (S.I. Historical Society), and the S.I. Zoo. The S.I. Institute of Arts & Sciences' permission to use illustrations from the S.I. Walk Book (1962) is greatly appreciated. It is a fitting way to remember the work of Mathilde Weingartner and Olive Earle.

I applaud the personal commitment of Ellen Pratt, Elsa Haas, Hillel Lofaso and other members of Protectors' Marketing Committee for all that you did to make this book a success. A special appreciation to Ellen Pratt for all her support from the beginning of this book's conception to its completion, and for her leadership and personal role in saving so many parks.

Without Protectors of Pine Oak Woods and all its members, thousands of acres of Staten Island would now be under pavement. It is because of caring and committed people like you that Staten Island is a better place for all generations.

I am indebted to Dick Buegler for his two years of loyalty, wisdom, and cheerful and patient support in every aspect of this book. You helped make this book a reality, just as you have brought to reality the creation of so many of the parks that this book showcases. You have left a shining legacy for all Staten Islanders, human and wild.

Thank you, my parents, Pearl and Morris Kershner, for fostering the love for Nature that has enriched my life. To my wife Helene, thank you for giving me the freedom, love and understanding through the years it took to create this book.

Lastly, thank you to Mother Nature and her Creator for giving us these treasures of nature at our doorstep and for making our world full of wonder and reverence.

*   *   *   *   *   *

This book is dedicated to the memory of my father, Morris Kershner, whose love of Staten Island's Greenbelt lives in these pages.

PREFACE

Secret Places of Staten Island is a dream come true... our dream, Bruce Kershner's dream, Protectors' dream. *Secret Places* is a gift to us on Staten Island, to our nature lovers and environmentalists, our residents, our children and teachers, as well as our builders, developers, city planners and public officials. It is a gift to our wildlife, our magnificent trees and exquisite wildflowers.

This guide celebrates our beautiful home, Staten Island, the home of our predecessors, our present neighbors, and our future citizens. *Secret Places* beckons us to the out-of-doors, to visit and be inspired, to learn and enjoy. In this book, we read about a secret place, see sketches and photos of it, follow clear directions to reach the scenic treasure, then navigate unfamiliar territory using handy maps. Finally, we step back to appreciate glorious nature.

Staten Island possesses extraordinary natural beauty in a large variety of interconnected ecosystems. For 150 years, our Island's naturalists were intrigued and inspired by this natural heritage. They focused their studies on natural history at the S.I. Institute of Arts and Sciences, ever since its founding in 1881. Their work initiated community discussion and efforts to preserve much of what still remains. We are challenged to claim that natural heritage as our own, and to come to its defense.

Protectors' advocacy -- the work of committed citizens -- was instrumental in acquiring Clay Pit Ponds, the Greenbelt, Corson Brook Woods, Blue Heron, Kingfisher and Long Ponds, St. Francis Woodlands, Mt. Loretto-by-the-Sea and many other green spaces.

Bruce Kershner's *Secret Places* can be seen as the culmination of decades of preservation efforts of Protectors of Pine Oak Woods and fellow organizations. It is the fulfillment of Protectors' obligation to the home community we have served for 25 years. It promises more preservation, more education, and more campaigns to save what remains of that natural heritage ... forever.

We hope you, too, will become involved. Join Protectors of Pine Oak Woods. Share with us your love of what you have experienced. Allow your wanderings in nature to broaden and enrich your life. *Never forget that nature's beauty is the most important part of our Staten Island heritage.*

Let this guide, *Secret Places of Staten Island*, enrich you, inspire you, and empower you to preserve and protect our Island's natural treasures.

For Protectors of Pine Oak Woods,
Dick Buegler and Ellen Pratt

FOREWORD

In his foreword to a *Sand County Almanac*, the visionary naturalist, Aldo Leopold, wrote that "there are some who can live without wild things, and some who cannot."

A half century has passed since those words were first recorded and a lot has changed. Today, our skies are more polluted, our waters more contaminated, and our cities more congested. On the positive side, we reach the millennium with a far clearer understanding of the environmental consequences of our actions. With all the threats that we continue to pose to our natural surroundings, and the comprehension of the effects of those threats, we can no longer afford to believe that wild things are a matter of taste.

"Wild things," as Leopold called them, are an integral part of the world in which we live, not just because of their natural beauty and their aesthetic value to humans, but because of their place in the delicate ecosystems that compose our living earth. Every time we clear a forest, build a road through a meadow, or dump our waste into our rivers and oceans, we endanger the plants and animals that live around us, and thereby endanger ourselves.

Some still believe that New York City, America's largest steel and concrete metropolis, is an exception to this rule. They are wrong. There are wild things here within North America's largest city, and we cannot live without them. New York City, in fact, shelters almost 28,000 acres of park land -- the largest urban park system in America -- and its green spaces harbor thousands of species of plants, birds and animals, including the endangered peregrine falcon, piping plover, least tern, giant yellow hyssop and loggerhead turtle.

The Borough of Staten Island is home to some of New York City's most fantastic and awesome natural treasures. With just under 7,000 acres of park land -- almost 18% of the entire borough -- it is second only to the much larger borough of Queens in "green" acreage. At the heart of the island lies the almost 3,000-acre Greenbelt. Its salt and freshwater wetlands, vast grasslands and oak barrens, moist forests of sweet gum, red maple and white ash, and oak-hickory uplands comprise a 4.5-square mile jewel. Staten Island also shelters the picturesque Blue Heron Park, a 222-acre forest of sweet gums, splashed with colorful wildflowers, tranquil ponds, and a vital expanse of watershed. Combined with wooded Wolfe's Pond Park, sandy Conference House Park, forested and wetland-rich Kingfisher Pond Park, undulating Clove Lakes Park and a variety of other natural gems, these green spaces make Staten Island a crucial sanctuary for New York City's wild things.

Wild things in Staten Island are very much the subject of *Secret Places of Staten Island.* It is a user's guide, intended to direct the reader through some of Staten Island's familiar green spots and into some of the author's more "secret places" on the island. Its goal is to induce an appreciation of Staten Island's natural spots in the reader. But there is another, more important, underlying message here. To continue to appreciate the natural beauty of New York City, we must all make a greater effort to preserve it for our children. City of New York/Parks and Recreation strives to do just that. Parks acquired over 1,200 acres of park land citywide between 1994 and 1997, and more than 1,000 of them were located in Staten Island. Many of these are delicate salt and fresh water marsh lands -- the so-called "kidneys" of the local ecosystem -- which protect the environment with their remarkable ability to absorb flood flows, prevent erosion and filter and biodegrade pollutants.

As you turn the pages of this guide, and venture into the "secret places" of the parks and preserves of Staten Island, remember that you are a visitor, a guest in the home of New York City's wild things. Treat them with respect and responsibility, and they will continue to be here to bring us balance and beauty for years to come.

Henry J. Stern
Commissioner
City of New York/Parks & Recreation

Von Briesen Park vista (1962), from the *S.I. Walk Book*

"I do exceedingly enjoy the view, sometimes it is wondrously beautiful ... I'm sure you would like Staten Island."
- Native Staten Islander, Frederick Law Olmsted, creator of Central Park, U.S. Capitol grounds and 180 other parks, 1848

"Looking Oceanward from Todt Hill" (1895) painting by Jasper Cropsey (1823-1900). Courtesy S.I. Institute of Arts & Sciences

Secret Places

INTRODUCTION

Staten Island possesses a wealth of scenic treasures. However, New Yorkers kiddingly remark about Staten Island that "no one really lives there" and that there is nothing of interest on Staten Island. People who don't live on Staten Island know it primarily as the place "where the ferry goes" and as a quick highway route from Long Island to New Jersey. Even most Staten Islanders view it as a pleasant -- but unremarkable -- bedroom community.

Well, the "secret is out!" New Yorkers no longer have the excuse to believe these myths. Staten Islanders and New Yorkers can now relish Staten Island's unique assets.

Instead of seeing Staten Island as "the lightly populated borough," it can now be seen as "heavily populated" -- with birdlife, wildflowers and impressive woods. Instead of being thought of as "relatively undeveloped," it can now be known as "highly developed" -- with rich wetland ecosystems, century-old forests and one of the country's largest urban parks. Rather than a place where "nothing is happening," it can be realized for its "outdoor happenings": the great monarch butterfly migration, the hawk-watching spectacle at Mt. Moses, the seasonal Greenbelt walks by Protectors, and the historical re-enactments at Richmond Town and Fort Wadsworth. Instead of being "unremarkable," you will be eager to remark about the only natural 360-degree panorama in NY City; the tallest ocean-facing cliff in NY State; haunted hills and strange fort ruins, and the classic panorama from the southernmost tip of NY State.

Where else can you see NY City's only historical village, and the oldest schoolhouse in America; mysterious rock inscriptions, and some of the largest and most ancient living things in NY City? Staten Island is the place where you can get inspired by its "necklace of panoramas," thrill at the sight of great blue herons or flocks of white egrets, or get mellowed out on a canoe trip through wild bayous.

Most remarkable of all is Staten Island's Greenbelt, a 3000-acre natural treasure with 18 ponds, exquisite forests, clear babbling brooks and a 35-mile foot trail network crossed by only a few roads.

One of the purposes of this book is to put Staten Island -- finally -- "on the map" of metro area dwellers. Staten Islanders can now appreciate the natural treasures in their own backyard, and everybody can see Staten Island as "an easy getaway destination," all of it reachable by public transportation! Staten Island is a place where you can leave the stress and hustle of city life behind ... on a quiet windswept hilltop, along a wild lily-padded pond, or under the green cathedral of an ancient woodland.

By publicizing Staten Island's treasures, "Once the secret's out, it's no longer a secret." If more people visit them, there is concern about their being degraded. As a life-long environmentalist, the author fully acknowledges this dilemma. I selected the places in this book because they can handle extra foot traffic. However, there is also a benefit. If more people visit these treasures, they will fall in love with them as I have. By expanding the core of people who visit and enjoy these treasures, we grow the constituency of citizens who will watch out for and care about our parks.

It is only because of caring and committed citizens, especially Protectors of Pine Oak Woods, that thousands of acres of Greenbelt, Bluebelt and other parks and natural areas were saved from the bulldozer. Staten Island's scenic and historic treasures are relentlessly threatened by people more interested in profits and exploitation than in protecting the public's quality of life -- or wildlife. Most of the sights in this book would not exist if ordinary people had not rallied to prevent their destruction from planned highways, commercial strips, uninterrupted housing development, and industrial "parks."

This is the first-ever comprehensive guide to Staten Island's scenic sights. Most of the places in this book have never previously appeared in print. I am proud that eight of these sights are totally new, that is, just purchased as public park land or just opened to the public for the first time. That's why we call them "secret places."

When you visit *your* scenic treasures, remember to show you care by following the simple rules: **"Leave only footprints, take only pictures, and kill only time."** Take a plastic bag so you can pick up litter dropped by uncaring people. Discourage defacement of trees or picking of wildflowers. Report dumping or illegal use of off-road vehicles. Join one of the organizations that work to protect parks -- they've already helped save many of the ones you enjoy. They welcome everybody on their scheduled walks, tours or wildlife watching trips. Write to public officials to urge them to fund and protect the existing parks, and to set aside unprotected natural treasures threatened by development.

Here are a few of the Island's "secret" places that could be lost unless citizens act: Willow Oak Woods, Annadale Triangle, Kreischer Hill, Graniteville Swamp, Northshore Greenbelt, and natural areas of Spanish Camp, Northern Seaview and Farm Colony. The Greenbelt still is threatened by proposed highways that need to be "de-mapped."

Remember that the job of caring about and fighting to protect our scenic wonders ultimately falls upon the people who know and care about them. These treasures are here for you to enjoy.

May your lives be enriched forever by the experience.

How to Find Staten Island's Secret Places

To find Staten Island's scenic wonders, you must follow both the driving and walking directions in this book. Bring the book with you. Read the directions and map at every turn. Otherwise, you may not find your scenic treasure, or get lost. We call them "secret places" because no signs tell you which way to go! Until this book was written, most of these sights were known only to a privileged few.

Know How to Read Trail Blazes:

- a single blaze means you are following the marked trail
- two blazes (one blaze is diagonally above the other) signal the trail is about to turn sharply. The "lean" of the upper blaze tells you the way to turn.
- three same-color blazes in a triangle pattern means you have reached the end of the trail.
- never cross a trail intersection without confirming that you are following the correct color blaze.
- if you find yourself on the wrong trail, return to the last intersection to check the blazes. USE YOUR MAP!

Safety Cautions

Staten Island certainly has wild woods filled with wildlife.

But for all you city slickers: there are no lions and tigers and bears (Oh my!) in Staten Island's woods. There are also **NO POISONOUS SNAKES**. It is far more hazardous to walk New York City's streets because of those dangerous *two-legged* animals! Rats and unleashed dogs are the next most dangerous animals in the city.

In the woods of Staten Island, there are only two "wild creatures" worth emphasizing from a safety standpoint: poison ivy and ticks. Once you know how to avoid them, the risk from their hazards is truly minimal. Just take these sensible precautions. Then go out and explore to your heart's delight.

Poison Ivy

Poison ivy generates much more fear than is worth it. It is not "evil" and it does not grab you. In fact, the irritating oil (called urushiol) probably prevents insects from eating its leaves. It is simply a coincidence that it contains an oil to which some humans react. It's no different from being allergic to milk or strawberries, except that those you eat instead of just touch. Once you know how

Secret Places　　　　　3

to recognize it and avoid it, it becomes only a routine concern in the outdoors.  **"Three Leaves, Let It Be."** Poison ivy has oval leaflets in threes, about one to three inches long. They are sometimes edged with one to three blunt "teeth" or none at all. They are sometimes glossy or have a reddish tinge to their leaf stalks or young leaves. It grows as a shrub or a vine. Its favorite place to grow is in *thickets, moist young woods, rocky places and shores*. It is least common in mature forests (such as featured in this book).

You cannot get poison ivy unless you *physically contact* it (or pet your dog who ran through it). To prevent it, simply know what it looks like and avoid it. Don't brush up against overhanging leaves, such as along narrow trails. The easiest way to get it is to walk *off-trail* through dense vegetation. Wash your clothes if exposed.

Not everyone who touches it, gets it (20% are immune to it). Most people require *multiple* exposures before reacting to it. The reaction doesn't start until 18 - 36 hours later. Soap will NOT remove it. If you know you touched it, you can remove it only within the *first hour* and only by *flooding* it with water (such as shower, bath, or jumping in a pond). Do not scratch poison ivy -- it will make it even more itchy and last even longer. Treat mild cases with calamine lotion. For stronger reactions, ask your pharmacist for the right over-the-counter ointment. For severe cases, see your doctor!

The most scientific, up-to-date source is *Nature's Revenge, Secrets of Poison Ivy*, by Susan Hauser (Lyons & Burford Publ., 1996).

Ticks

Dog ticks are common in the metro area. They are the size of a wooden match head. Though obnoxious, **dog ticks are NOT carriers of Lyme disease**. Ticks begin to bite 12 to 24 hours later. They are not active in cold weather.

The tiny deer tick (size of a sesame seed) appears to be rare on Staten Island. It carries Lyme disease, a long-term bacterial infection.

To avoid ticks: 1) stay on trails (note: mature open forests, such as those featured in this book, are poor habitat for ticks); 2) avoid brushing past grassy or scrubby vegetation along the trail; 3) dress in long pants, tucked into socks; 4) spray your pants and hands with bug repellent if you have to brush against vegetation; 4) when you get home, inspect your body. Remove ticks with a tweezers.

For more information, contact the NY State Dept. of Health, ESP, Corning Tower, Rm. 651, Albany, NY 12237-0627.

STATEN ISLAND'S NECKLACE OF PANORAMAS

Take the Grand Driving Tour of Staten Island's world-class panoramas. Start at that most famous of all -- the unsurpassed vista of Manhattan and New York Harbor from the Ferry Terminal. Stand before the same vistas that inspired Romantic-era artists to paint these scenes, which now hang in museums. See sweeping views from high hills and wild shores, from sharp bluffs and from the southernmost tip of New York State.

Distance: All the panoramas in this tour are roadside views or only five-minute walks. The driving distance, if you do the entire route, is 23.7 miles.

Level of Difficulty: easy

Things to Bring: a desire to be inspired and a love of beauty; camera, binoculars, and of course, clear viewing weather (summer haze is the least desirable season).

"The whole island is like a garden, and affords very fine scenery." *Henry David Thoreau, 1843*

New York City abounds with grand views -- from bridges, skyscrapers, harborfronts. However, Staten Island offers a gourmet menu of vistas not possible from the rest of the metro area. It is the only place that offers this combination: it lies directly in front of the commanding Manhattan skyline, yet also faces country views where you can't imagine you're in a city at all. Being an island, it offers views from its shoreline, but it is also the only borough with scenes from atop wild hill summits. Millions of tourists adore the incredible harbor views from Staten Island's own ferry. But few New Yorkers are aware of the city's only 360-degree long-distance panorama (Mt. Moses) that is not atop a building, tower or bridge.

The Tour of Staten Island's Necklace of Panoramas

This tour takes you along a string of pearls, from one roadside vista to another. Along the way, it also offers you the choice to get out and visit other stunning vistas reached only on foot.
The S.I. Ferry Terminal Panorama "Everybody" knows about the classical vista from the deck of the Staten Island Ferry as it travels back and forth from Manhattan. Those views of the entire harbor include the Statue of Liberty, the skyline, and all the distant bridges. But you don't have to take the ferry to see this. The best street view is from the harbor side of Richmond Terrace where it meets the Ferry Terminal entrance ramp. Finding parking is a prob-

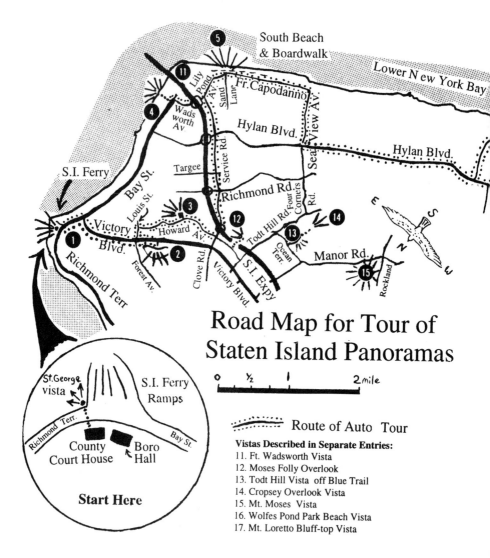

Road Map for Tour of Staten Island Panoramas

South Beach & Boardwalk

Lower New York Bay

Ft.Capodanno

Hylan Blvd.

Hylan Blvd.

S.I. Ferry

Targee

Richmond Rd.

Victory

Howard

Blvd.

Manor Rd.

0   ½   1   2 mile

St.George vista

S.I. Ferry Ramps

County Court House   Boro Hall

Start Here

⋯⋯⋯ Route of Auto Tour

Vistas Described in Separate Entries:
11. Ft. Wadsworth Vista
12. Moses Folly Overlook
13. Todt Hill Vista off Blue Trail
14. Cropsey Overlook Vista
15. Mt. Moses Vista
16. Wolfes Pond Park Beach Vista
17. Mt. Loretto Bluff-top Vista

lem, though. On the weekend, parking along Richmond Terrace is possible. You can also look for a spot on Hyatt Street up the hill.

To locate exactly where the best street vista is, stand in front of the County Courthouse (next to Borough Hall, which is opposite the Ferry Terminal). Cross Richmond Terrace and head to the corner situated on the *left edge* of the Ferry Terminal access ramps.

This 180-degree view starts on the far left with the Watchung Mountains (a very distant long ridge visible on clear days). Moving to the right are Jersey City's skyline (across the Kill Van Kull channel that forms the Island's north shore). Ellis Island and the Statue of Liberty appear next, followed by Manhattan's skyline. With binoculars, you can separate the Brooklyn Bridge from the Manhattan and

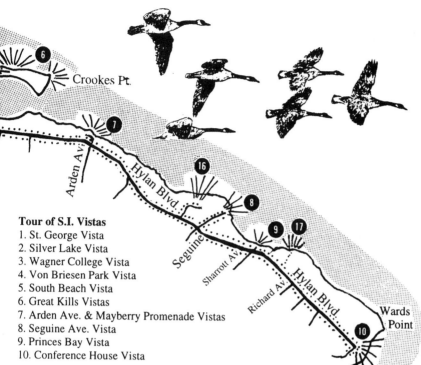

Crookes Pt.

Tour of S.I. Vistas
1. St. George Vista
2. Silver Lake Vista
3. Wagner College Vista
4. Von Briesen Park Vista
5. South Beach Vista
6. Great Kills Vistas
7. Arden Ave. & Mayberry Promenade Vistas
8. Seguine Ave. Vista
9. Princes Bay Vista
10. Conference House Vista

Arden Av.

Hylan Blvd

Seguine

Sharrott Av.

Richard Av.

Hylan Blvd

Wards Point

Williamsburg Bridges. The skyscrapers of Brooklyn Heights are next, followed by Brooklyn's industrial waterfront. Last to the right is Greenwood Cemetery (the thin green strip of trees just before the vista ends), Brooklyn's highest point.

In the harbor, notice Robin's Reef (Dutch for Seal Reef) and its conical light house, built 1883. Count how many kinds of boats you can see: ferries, tug boats, barges, tankers, sailboats, motorboats, containerships, cruise liners, maybe even the Sloop Clearwater.

For a guided tour of the panorama, call the S.I. Institute of Arts & Sciences, 718-727-1135.

From St. George Terminal, drive south on Bay Street. Turn right on Victory Blvd. When the road climbs to the top of the ridge, pass Forest Avenue on your right and immediately find parking along Victory Blvd.

The Silver Lake Vista Walk to the corner of Forest and Victory Blvd. Look down Victory Blvd. to see the twin towers of the World Trade Center "floating" in the distance. Head 1,000 feet south (away from Manhattan) along Victory Blvd.

Opposite 630 Victory Blvd., a row of six stone and red brick apartments, is the Silver Lake Park **vista**. Stroll down the promenade to the upper overlook terrace. Here is the Island's best hilltop view

St. George Vista

Northwest

New Jersey

Watchung Range (16 mi. away)

Newark Skyline (11 mi. away)

North

Jersey City Skyline (6 mi. away)

Ellis Is.(processed millions of immigrants, now Ntl. Park)

Constables Hook

Rockefeller Plaza (9 mi. away)

Empire State Bldg. (1300' tall)

World Finan. Ctr. Bldgs.

World Trade Ctr. 1500' tall

Bayonne

Kill Van Kull

water tower

Greenville Automanna Terminal (loads military ships)

Robbins Reef - Light House

Statue of Liberty (300', tallest statue in world, built 1886)

across New Jersey. To your left is a radio tower and Todt Hill (the Island's highest hill and the highest point on the Atlantic seaboard south of Maine -- see page 42). The next hill is in Clove Lakes Park. Trees partly obscure the arch of the Bayonne Bridge. To the right of the Silver Lake causeway begins the distant view of New Jersey. The long ridge is Watchung Mountain, 16 miles away. Below the ridge are New Jersey's industry row and Newark Airport (with binoculars, watch the jets taking off), and part of Newark's skyline.

The 58-acre Silver Lake is the terminus of the Catskill water supply for New York City. The 107-acre park offers jogging, walking and biking trails past ornamental plantings, as well as a golf course. The South Basin is a favorite for bird watchers.

Return to the junction of Victory Blvd. and Forest Avenue. Across from Forest Avenue is Louis Street. Turn up this steep road, then make the first right onto Howard Avenue. Drive past classic elegant homes (with their own private vistas). After many sharp curves, look for the vista as it appears to your left. Park along Howard Avenue on your left where there is a break in the hedges. You can also turn left into the entrance road to the beautiful Wagner College campus. Ask the gatehouse guard for permission to park in the lot just to see the vista.

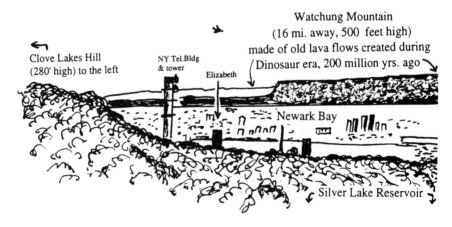

Watchung Mountain
(16 mi. away, 500 feet high)
made of old lava flows created during
Dinosaur era, 200 million yrs. ago

Clove Lakes Hill (280' high) to the left

NY Tel.Bldg & tower

Elizabeth

Newark Bay

Silver Lake Reservoir

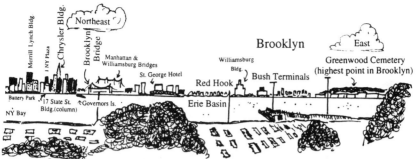

Manhattan

Merrill Lynch Bldg / I NY Plaza / Chrysler Bldg. / Brooklyn Bridge / Northeast / Brooklyn / East / Manhattan & Williamsburg Bridges / St. George Hotel / Williamsburg Bldg. / Bush Terminals / Greenwood Cemetery (highest point in Brooklyn) / Battery Park / 17 State St. Bldg.(column) / Governors Is. / NY Bay / Red Hook / Erie Basin

The Wagner College Vista You are atop Grymes Hill, famous for its bay views. Across the blue strip of Upper New York Bay is Brooklyn's Bay Ridge. The entire graceful span of the Verrazano Narrows Bridge accents this vista. Under the bridge are the reddish Fox Hills Apartments on Staten Island, as well as Gravesend Bay. Coney Island (seven miles away) is to the bridge's right. Can you see the old parachute jump and Ferris wheel? The view ends with Lower New York Bay stretching far away.

> "God might have made a more beautiful spot, but never did."
> *An oft-quoted Colonial era saying inspired by*
> *this famous bay scene atop Grymes Hill*

Return to Howard Avenue and continue on. At the bottom of the steep hill, turn left on Clove Road. (Note: you are very close to the parking spot for the start of the **Todt Hill** hike, described on p. 42. Within the first 500 feet of this hike, after a steep climb, you can see the **vista from Moses' Folly** overpass.) Cross over the S.I. Expressway, then turn left and follow the service road along the side of the Expressway. The service road crosses Richmond Road and then crosses Targee Street. Next, it feeds you onto the entrance to the Expressway on the left. Notice the highway view of the Verrazano Bridge as you near it. Take the Bay

Northwest

Silver Lake Park Vista

Newark Airport / City of Newark / Port of Newark Containerport

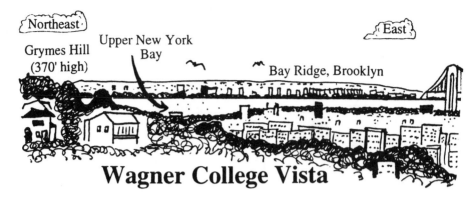

Northeast

Upper New York Bay

Grymes Hill (370' high)

East

Bay Ridge, Brooklyn

Wagner College Vista

street exit (last one before the bridge). Turn left on Lily Pond Avenue, then turn right onto Wadsworth Avenue. It ends at Bay Street. The parking lot for Von Briesen Park is directly in front of you.

Von Briesen Park Vista (illustrated in Foreword, p.*ix*) Walk up the hill along the paved path. Von Briesen Park was an old estate donated by that family in 1849. Arthur Von Briesen's house was the first home in America that 19th century immigrants could see from ships approaching Upper New York Bay. This inspired one person to write a post card simply addressed "First House on the Left, America" -- and it was actually delivered to the Von Briesens!

Enjoy the unusual trees that this park is noted for -- bald cypress, European beech, English oak, empress tree, mulberry, Japanese pagoda tree. The park's vista is especially romantic, with its close-up view of the Verrazano Bridge, Brooklyn's Bay Ridge, and Manhattan's skyline to the left. This peaceful place is perfect for shedding the rush of the city while you watch the cruise ships, tankers and other ships pass quietly below you. (If weeds block the view, call the Parks Department 718-390-8000 to clear it.)

bald cypress

If you want to tour **Fort Wadsworth**, which has an even better panorama, its entrance is next to Von Briesen Park, through the gate at the end of Bay Street (see page 99).

From Von Briesen Park, drive across Bay Street back onto Wadsworth Avenue. When it ends, turn left and follow Lily Pond Avenue under the Expressway. Continue on it to Father Capodanno Blvd. Drive a short distance to the intersection with Sand Lane and pull to the left into the beach parking lot.

South Beach Panorama Few people realize that the Franklin Roosevelt Boardwalk along South Beach is the world's fourth longest. This boardwalk and the beach offer a vista with a different angle of the Verrazano Bridge -- from the south. The bridge is to the left with **Fort Wadsworth** below it. Across Lower New York Bay

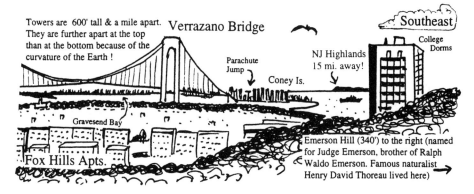

Towers are 600' tall & a mile apart. **Verrazano Bridge**
They are further apart at the top
than at the bottom because of the
curvature of the Earth !

Parachute
Jump

NJ Highlands
15 mi. away!

Coney Is.

College
Dorms

Gravesend Bay

Fox Hills Apts.

Emerson Hill (340') to the right (named
for Judge Emerson, brother of Ralph
Waldo Emerson. Famous naturalist
Henry David Thoreau lived here)

are Gravesend Bay and Coney Island, with its rows of tall apartment buildings. On a clear day, the Marine Parkway Bridge and Rockaway Point (another part of Gateway National Recreation Area) may be seen to the right of Coney Island, five miles away.

Look for the two small offshore islands to your right. They are Hoffman and Swinburne Islands, now also part of Gateway Recreation Area. They were once quarantine centers where patients with infectious diseases were sent, 75 to 100 years ago. They are still off-limits because they are now sensitive bird nesting areas.

Far out to the right, 14 miles away, you may sight New Jersey's Sandy Hook and Atlantic Highlands.

To continue to the next grand vista, turn left on Father Capodanno Blvd. At Seaview Avenue, turn right. Turn left on Hylan Blvd. Drive 2.6 miles to Great Kills Park's entrance. (To view the Island's finest Greenbelt vistas, see **Mt. Moses' "Million Dollar Vista"** (p.74) and the **classical Jasper Cropsey Vista** (p. 47)).

The Great Kills Panorama The view here is similar to the one from South Beach, except you can see Manhattan and more of New Jersey is visible. The World Trade Center looms to the left over trees (not water). On a clear day, the Long Island's Marine Parkway Bridge and Far Rockaway can be seen (20 miles away). Notice the lighthouse in front of Sandy Hook, the very low strip to the southeast in New Jersey. See if you can sight the twin light house on the crest of the Atlantic Highlands. (If you are interested in hiking to the end of Great Kills Park, read page 109.)

"The sea beach is the best thing I have seen. It is very solitary and remote, and you only remember New York occasionally. The distances, too, along the shore and inland in sight of it, are unaccountably great and startling."
Naturalist Henry David Thoreau, describing Staten Island, 1843

Return to Hylan Blvd. and turn left. (Along the way, you will pass the turnoffs for **Kingfisher Pond and Wood Duck Pond** (page 127) and for the

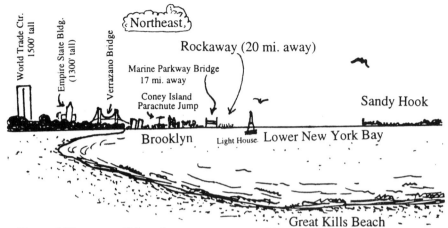

Olmsted Homestead historic trees -- see page 21.)

     After 2.3 miles on Hylan, turn left on Arden Avenue. A little-known ocean vista is at the end of Arden Avenue and from Mayberry Promenade (turn left at the end of Arden). Return to Hylan and turn left. Along the way, you pass Poillon Avenue that takes you to **Blue Heron Park**; see page 135. In 1.6 miles, pass the entrance to **Wolfe's Pond Park**. In this park, there's a fine vista from its beach, as well as an outstanding walk (page 110). Just after the park is Seguine Avenue. Turn left on Seguine and drive to its end for your seventh vista.

    The Seguine Avenue Vista offers a view of Princes Bay and the red bluffs of Mt. Loretto. As you drive along Seguine, you also pass the **Historic Olmsted Grove of Osage Oranges**, including the State Champion Tree (page 22). From the shore, you can look inland and see the stately, historic **Seguine House**, built in 1840.

    Return to Hylan Blvd., turn left and drive 3/4 mile to Sharrott Avenue.

    Sharrott Avenue Vista Turn left on Sharrott Avenue. At the end is a close view of the dramatic red clay **bluffs of Mt. Loretto**. You can choose to walk down the beach to the bluffs (see page 114).

Conference House Vista

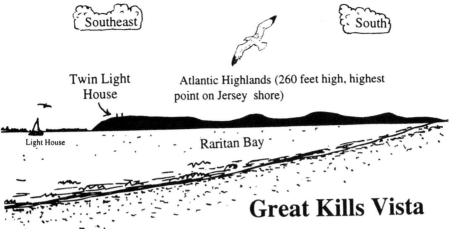

Twin Light House

Atlantic Highlands (260 feet high, highest point on Jersey shore)

Light House

Raritan Bay

Great Kills Vista

Return to Hylan Blvd. Again, go left. Within 1/4 mile, pass the immaculate meadows of Mt. Loretto and reach Richard Avenue. (If you wish to climb **Mt. Loretto's bluffs** (page 114) or explore **Long Pond** (page 140), park here.) As you drive along Hylan Blvd., you will pass Page Avenue and Sprague Avenue (where you can visit three **Great and Historic Trees**; see page 22-23). Continue on Hylan Blvd. to its end. Turn right on Satterlee Street and park.

Conference House Panorama Walk to the entrance to Conference House Park. Visit the famous **Conference House** and its two **historic trees** (described on page 23). Walk to the beach. This panorama is different from all previous ones because you can see Perth Amboy and the Raritan River, as well as New Jersey's Atlantic Highlands and Sandy Hook, 15 miles away. If you wish to walk the beach to the southernmost tip of New York State, read page 120.

> "The prospect of the country here is extremely pleasing ....
> Hills and vallies still continued ... to change alternately."
> *Naturalist Peter Kalm, describing Staten Island in 1748*

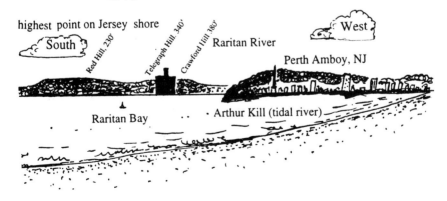

highest point on Jersey shore

South

Red Hill, 230'

Telegraph Hill, 340'

Crawford Hill, 380'

Raritan River

West

Perth Amboy, NJ

Raritan Bay

Arthur Kill (tidal river)

Staten Island's Legacy of Naturalists

Not only is Staten Island rich in scenic treasures, it also has a rich history and legacy of famous naturalists. Because it has so much natural beauty so close to the center of a great city, it has spawned or attracted a wonderfully disproportionate number of naturalists. These naturalists, whether they are philosophers, scientists, photographers or scholars of nature, have left a permanent mark because of their inspired words, leadership or scientific contributions. Here is a too-brief sampling of this proud legacy.

• **Henry David Thoreau**, one of the world's most famous naturalists, lived in Staten Island in 1843 where he wrote "the whole island is like a garden and affords very fine scenery." He lived with Judge William Emerson (for which Emerson Hill was named). Judge Emerson was the brother of the renowned poet **Ralph Waldo Emerson**, who also lived with Judge Emerson for periods of time.

• **Nathaniel Lord Britton** (1859-1934), one of the most famous American botanists, lived in Staten Island from 1859 to 1915. He was the founder and first director of the NY Botanical Gardens and co-founded the S.I. Institute of Arts & Sciences. He authored one of the "Bibles" of botany, a 3-volume guide to all of the higher plants of northeast North America. You can now visit his historic homestead in Richmond Town (p.89,98).

• **Frederick Law Olmsted** (1822 - 1903) is the "Father of Landscape Architecture," and the creator of Central Park, Brooklyn's Prospect Park and 160 parks from Boston to San Francisco. He was the first to conceive of a greenbelt of parks on Staten Island and the first two Greenbelt trails are called the "Olmsted Trailway." His historic home is the 1690 **Akerly Farm** (p.21), now the residence where Staten Island's current naturalist emeritus, **Carleton Beil**, lives. Mr. Beil is a well-known naturalist who for many years was an educator at the American Museum of Natural History in NY City.

• **William T. Davis** (1862-1945) is one of the most famous insect authorities (and the world's expert on the 17-year cicada). He also co-founded Staten Island's oldest cultural institution, the S.I. Institute of Arts and Sciences (which includes the museum collections). His book, *Days Afield on Staten Island*, is an elegant and poetic reminiscence of natural Staten Island before the era of urban sprawl. He is commemorated by the name of the William T. Davis Wildlife Refuge, which he established.

• **Howard Cleaves**, the world's first professional wildlife photographer (1887-1981), pioneered wildlife photography techniques that are now standard. He was the first to photograph animals at night and first to photograph the Galapagos Islands.

• **Mathilde Weingartner** (1907 - 1989), long-time educator and curator for the S.I. Institute of Arts & Sciences, inspired thousands of children and adults through decades of her nature programs. She wrote the first profile of Staten Island's parks, a booklet, *The Staten Island Walk Book,* whose illustrations are pictured in this book.

• This rich legacy is being continued by living naturalists and environmental leaders. **John G. Mitchell**, co-founder of Staten Island's first Greenbelt protection organization, is now a nationally famous nature author and senior editor for National Geographic Society. Biologist, **Dr. Arthur Shapiro**, after living on the Island for several years, left his mark with *New York City's Last Frontier: Field Trips on Staten Island*, a description of rare plant and wildlife habitats (many of which have been saved through the efforts of Protectors of Pine Oak Woods). Many other current Staten Island natural scientists and environmental leaders continue contributing to Staten Island's great legacy. But two, in particular, need to be cited:

• **Richard Buegler** and **Ellen Pratt** have been Staten Island's foremost environmental leaders for decades. Buegler is a co-founder of Protectors of Pine Oak Woods and both are leaders of this highly successful environmental organization. They have been in the forefront of the struggles that have successfully saved thousands of acres of Staten Island's natural treasures. They have individually been recognized for their leadership with one of the nation's most prestigious awards, the Feinstone Environmental Prize.

Henry David Thoreau

Frederick Law Olmsted

Nathaniel Lord Britton

William T. Davis

ON THE TRAIL OF THE GIANTS:
THE GREAT TREES OF STATEN ISLAND

Take a leisurely auto tour of the largest and oldest living things on Staten Island. Stand in awe under the borough's greatest tree. Meet other Champion Trees. Find out what it means to be "towering," "venerable," "massive," or even "gnarled." Put your arms around them to truly feel their size, and it's okay to hug them, too!

Distance: Walking distance is negligible, since all trees in this chapter are along a road or a short distance from one. Auto driving distance, if you travel the entire route, is 21 miles.

Level of Difficulty: Easy

Things to Bring: A love of trees (and your membership card in the Tree Huggers Society*); camera, tree guide

*There's no such thing, silly!

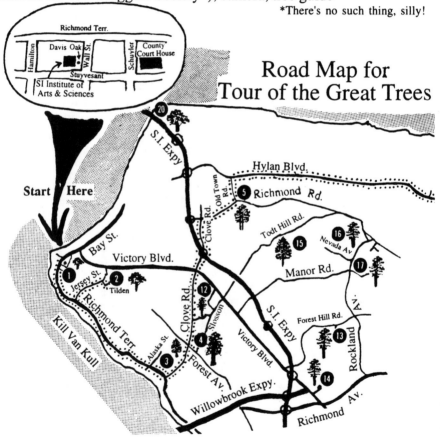

Road Map for Tour of the Great Trees

How to Appreciate the Great Trees

The first thing to recognize is that you are not going to see trees as large as giant redwoods. Trees with trunk diameters that are 10 feet or larger grow almost exclusively out west. In the northeastern U.S., trees more than four feet in diameter are notable, and trees with five- to six-foot wide trunks are as large as any ever get, with very few exceptions.

A second point is that some trees, like oaks, can grow impressively, but other kinds of trees are simply limited in their genetic ability to grow as large. As an example, the world's largest house cat is nowhere as big as a mountain lion (and I hope one never gets that large!).

To really appreciate these champion creatures, follow these guidelines:

• **You must walk up to its trunk. Put your hand on it and look up.** If you don't do this, you will never get a sense of its size since you have no human scale to compare it to. If you only stand ten feet away, you will miss the "greatness" of the tree.

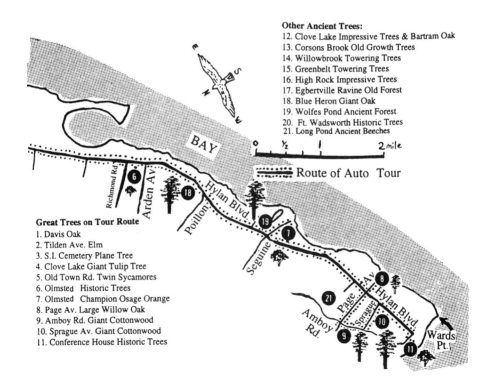

Other Ancient Trees:
12. Clove Lake Impressive Trees & Bartram Oak
13. Corsons Brook Old Growth Trees
14. Willowbrook Towering Trees
15. Greenbelt Towering Trees
16. High Rock Impressive Trees
17. Egbertville Ravine Old Forest
18. Blue Heron Giant Oak
19. Wolfes Pond Ancient Forest
20. Ft. Wadsworth Historic Trees
21. Long Pond Ancient Beeches

Route of Auto Tour

Great Trees on Tour Route
1. Davis Oak
2. Tilden Ave. Elm
3. S.I. Cemetery Plane Tree
4. Clove Lake Giant Tulip Tree
5. Old Town Rd. Twin Sycamores
6. Olmsted Historic Trees
7. Olmsted Champion Osage Orange
8. Page Av. Large Willow Oak
9. Amboy Rd. Giant Cottonwood
10. Sprague Av. Giant Cottonwood
11. Conference House Historic Trees

• The best way to gauge its true size is to see how many arm spreads it takes to go around the trunk. Besides, after centuries of enduring hurricanes and windstorms, lightning, disease, droughts and vandalism, wouldn't you want a hug, too?

• Observe how high it soars before reaching its first thick bough (for towering trees); for low-branched trees, notice how thick yet graceful its spreading boughs are.

• Observe other features, such as its buttressed roots (the bulging extensions at the base of the trunk), giant knots, lightning scars, or deep furrows or peeling plates on the bark.

The Trail of the Giants

The Trail of the Giants begins near the Staten Island Ferry.

Going north on Bay Street, pass by the entrance to the S.I. Ferry and Borough Hall, and continue along Richmond Terrace. Take the third left after Borough Hall (Hamilton Avenue). Drive up the steep hill one block. Turn left on Stuyvesant Place, and go one block, passing the S.I. Institute of Arts & Sciences (and museum). Turn left down Wall Street and pull off *immediately* along the side of the Museum building.

The Davis Oak Your tour starts off with a tree that is modest in size, but still a champion: the world's largest Davis Oak. It is a rare hybrid of black oak and willow oak (*Quercus philialis*). The tree was apparently planted by Staten Island's famous naturalist William T. Davis in about 1930.

Staten Island is unusual for its hybrid oaks. No one knows why they hybridize so well here. Hybridizing occurs when two different species mate and successfully set seed that contains the combined genes of the two different species -- like a horse and donkey.

While you are here, you may want to find long-term parking (along Hyatt Street or Richmond Terrace) and see Staten Island's oldest cultural institution, **the S.I. Institute of Arts and Sciences**, which is much more than it appears. Inside are quality exhibits of art and nature. It is also the hub of an extensive program of nature, science and art talks and shows, and is a meeting ground for Staten Island's nature lovers, environmentalists, birders, botanists, geologists and art lovers. For information or to join, contact them at 75 Stuyvesant Place, S.I. 10301, 718-727-1135.

From the S.I. Institute, drive 0.8 mile west on Richmond Terrace to Jersey Street. Make a left, drive 0.6 mile, and turn right on Brighton Street. Pass York Street; the next street off Brighton is Tilden Street.

Staten Island's Largest Elm   At the corner of
Tilden and Brighton Streets is Staten Island's **largest
elm** tree. What makes this four-foot, two-inch diameter
tree even more significant is that nearly all American elms
across the country have been killed by the Dutch elm
disease. Regal American elms once lined street after street
and were beloved because of their classical spreading,
towering wine-glass shape. This one is a lonely survivor.

Return to Richmond Terrace and turn left. Travel 1.8 miles (passing
Sailors Snug Harbor and the **S.I. Botanic Gardens** along the way). Four
blocks after Broadway is Alaska Street. Park on Alaska Street and walk back to
Richmond Terrace. Turn right, pass an industrial site and look for a business with
the address "1632" Richmond Terrace. Just before this is a woods road. Walk along
it into the grounds of the Staten Island Cemetery. Only 25 to 30 feet up the slope
is the giant tree on the right.

The City's Champion Plane Tree   Just inside the Staten Island
Cemetery is a five-foot, three-inch diameter **London plane tree**. It
is tied for being the city's largest. The plane tree is another old-
fashioned favorite street tree, especially because of its resistance to air
pollution. It is actually a hybrid of the American and the Oriental
sycamores. Notice its broad, many-pointed leaves. Its fruits are
sometimes called "fuzzy balls" and are well known to children who
toss them at each other. The old cemetery is fascinating to explore.

Continue west on Richmond Terrace several more blocks to Clove Road.
Turn left and drive nine blocks to Forest Avenue. Turn right and park a half-block
up, just before the forest strip on your left. Walk to the Clove Lakes Park side of
the road.

Staten Island's Largest Living Thing   Walk
down the park's paved walkway that parallels the edge
of the woods. Only 200 feet down the trail, notice the
huge tree in the meadow to your left. This is a **seven-
foot diameter tulip tree** (a kind of magnolia). It
stands about 107 feet high and at least 300 years old.
The tulip tree (also called "yellow poplar") is noted for
its large yellow flowers in spring, if you can see them
way up there! Admire how high it reaches to the first
bough. Look at its deeply furrowed bark, huge
buttressed roots, sheer massiveness, and the lightning
cable to protect it during storms. This tree started when the earliest
Dutch settlers arrived. Let's all hope it lives another several centuries!

(Note: see page 38-40 for a description of Clove Lakes Park's grove of **impressive trees** and also the world's **largest hybrid Bartram's oak**, a short distance from Victory Blvd.)

Largest living thing on Staten Island, Clove Lake's six-foot diameter tulip tree

Drive south on Clove Road, cross Victory Blvd., then cross over the S.I. Expressway. Turn left on the Clove Road extension until you reach Richmond Road. Turn right on Richmond Road and pass Doctors Hospital. About four or five blocks later, turn left on Old Town Road. Park immediately.

The Twin Sycamores On the left side of Old Town Road are **two stately sycamore trees**, perfectly straight and free of branches for a long way up. The one closest to Richmond Road is three feet, six inches in diameter; the other has a three-foot, ten-inch diameter. It took a citizen protest to prevent the cutting of these two beautiful trees. Notice their beautiful green and light brown flaky patches of bark.

(Between this and the next stop in southern Staten Island is the Greenbelt. Groves of **impressive trees** are found in Willowbrook Park (p.54), Corson Brook Woods (p.55), St. Francis (p.50), the Central Greenbelt (p.63), High Rock (p.67), and Egbertville Ravine (p.78). Fort Wadsworth (p.102) also has **two Great Trees**.)

Take Old Town Road south to Hylan Blvd. Turn right and drive five miles south to the next stop. You pass Great Kills Park, and later, Richmond *Avenue*. After you pass Richmond Avenue, park on Preston Avenue. Walk along Hylan Blvd. and watch for the house numbers. Between 4499 and 4521 Hylan Blvd., turn right onto a road-like driveway.

The Historic Trees of the Olmsted Homestead Walk up this driveway and turn onto the right fork. You are entering the ancient yard of the **Akerly Farm**, whose first section was built in 1690. It was the former Frederick Law Olmsted Homestead (it rhymes!). He is the Father of Landscape Architecture, the Father of Central Park and much more (see page 14).

When you enter the yard, you are on private property. It is a privilege to be allowed here. Show your respect and keep away from the old homestead.

In the yard is a collection of trees planted by Frederick Law Olmsted in the 1840s. The nearly four-foot diameter **cedar of Lebanon** has a plaque commemorating it. Olmsted transported 700 seeds of this Biblical tree from the Middle East and saved two for himself. Notice the graceful three-trunked tree in the yard -- it is the odd **osage orange** (detailed ahead). Olmsted's other large old trees are a Chinese **gingko** (a living fossil, found preserved in 300 million year-old rock); a **horsechestnut** (with palm-like leaves, large spring blossoms and prickle-covered nuts); **black walnut** (feathery leaves and edible, though tough-to-crack nuts); and **sycamore**.

Continue south along Hylan Blvd. another 1.2 miles. You pass Poillon Avenue (where Blue Heron Park is located, including its **Giant Old Oak**; see page 137). Later, you reach Wolfe's Pond Park's entrance (see page if you want to explore its **primeval forest** and giant trees; see page 110).

A half mile past Wolfe's Pond Park entrance is Seguine Avenue (pronounced "See-guy-n," as in "guy"). Turn left, drive one block and park.

The Olmsted Osage Oranges Locate 342 Seguine Avenue on your right (with a fenced-in yard -- **do not enter it!**). At the yard's corner is NY State's **Champion osage orange**, nearly four feet in diameter. In the 1840s, Frederick Law Olmsted planted this tree and the next three blocks of osage oranges (opposite S.I. University Hospital), all the way to the shore.

The osage orange is named after the bizarre "grapefruit" it produces in November; be sure to see these large, citrus-fragrant but otherwise inedible fruits. Its brilliant fall foliage is outstanding. The tree is actually a transplant from the Mississippi valley. It was brought east by farmers who knew it grew into a living fence, complete with thorns! (Note: near the end of Seguine Avenue is the historic, stately **Seguine House**, built in 1840.)

osage orange

Return to Hylan Blvd. and make a left (south). Drive 1.9 miles, passing picturesque **Mt. Loretto** (page 114) and **Long Pond Park** (p.140) At Page Avenue, turn left and drive to 750 Page Avenue, on your right.

The Page Avenue Willow Oak Along the street is a large specimen of an oak that is rare in NY State. The **willow oak** is a southern tree and reaches its northern limits here in NY City. This willow oak is nearly four feet in diameter. See if you can get a look at its leaves. Although it is an oak, its leaves resemble those of a willow!

willow oak

Drive across Hylan Blvd. and head north on Page Avenue. When Page Avenue reaches Amboy Road, turn left. Then pull immediately into the driveway of S.I. Savings Bank or the shopping center next to it.

The Amboy Road Cottonwood Walk across Amboy Road (**be careful of traffic!**) to the colossal tree on the other side. This five-foot, one-inch diameter **cottonwood** grows anonymously in a scrubby lot -- wonder who owns it? Approach it as closely as you can to get an idea of its size, but **watch for poison ivy**. The cottonwood has large triangular leaves that flop and quiver in the lightest breeze. It got its name from the large quantities of cotton-coated seeds that drop from it in June.

Continue south on Amboy Road (away from Page Avenue). Count four blocks on your left until you reach Sprague Avenue. Turn left and drive to George Street (on your right).

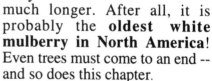

cottonwood

The City's Largest Cottonwood At the corner of George and Sprague is an even **larger cottonwood**, with a diameter of five feet, four inches. Remember to touch (or even hug) this grand old tree, which stands between the curb and the sidewalk.

Proceed south on Sprague Street, one block to Hylan Blvd. Turn right on Hylan and drive 3/4 mile to its end. Turn right at the end onto Satterlee Street. Drive one block and park.

The Conference House Historic Trees Walk to the entrance of **Conference House Park**. Ahead of you is one of the country's most historic homes, the **Conference House**, described on page 120. When you reach the historic house, look to your left at the stately **six-foot sycamore** standing alone in the yard. This tree with brown and green peeling patches on its bark is younger than the house, probably from the early 1800s.

white mulberry

Walk to the bay side of the house. Look at the gnarled, **ancient white mulberry** tree surrounded by a fence. This four-foot diameter mulberry is as old as the house (300 years old) but the tree may not be around much longer. After all, it is probably the **oldest white mulberry in North America**! Even trees must come to an end -- and so does this chapter.

For questions about trees, contact S.I. Institute of Arts & Sciences (718-727-1135), or Dr. Steve Clements, Brooklyn Botanical Garden (718-622-4433). Two recommended guides are _Trees: A Golden Guide_ (Western Publishing, 1990) and the _Audubon Society Field Guide to North American Trees_ (Alfred Knopf, Inc., 1980).

Credit: John Prasek

300-year old tulip tree at Clove Lake Park

MARINERS MARSH: STRANGE RUINS IN A POND-SPECKLED PRESERVE

Roam past giant, vine-smothered ruins that could be a scene out of "Raiders of the Lost Ark." Explore up to ten ponds and silently see what unusual wildlife awaits you. Climb atop fort-like ruins of Monument Pond for a vista. Enjoy the experience of seeing a real, still-surviving prairie, seemingly transported out of the Great Plains.

Distance: 1.8 mile round trip

Level of Difficulty: easy

Things to Bring: Dress for tick and bug protection. Bring a child-like joy in climbing rocks; proper foot gear (ground can be wet); binoculars, bird and flower guides, plastic bags to pick up litter. Know your poison ivy (common here).

Take normal crime safety precautions by going with a friend.

Scenic Delights:
Fortress-Like Ruins "Vine-covered ruins scattered across the site give you a sense that some long-lost civilization was swallowed up by the vegetation." That's how Howard Snyder of the Mariners Marsh Conservancy, describes it. Giant rectangular blocks, columns and pyramid-shaped "monuments" lie scattered about this preserve in seven areas. Full-sized trees grow in their cracks; vines drape down their sides. Emerging out of the forest, or standing mutely over the pond, you feel as if you stumbled upon ancient temple ruins.

Remember the old saying, "From a sow's ear to a silk purse"? This natural area is a testament to Nature's ability to reclaim an industrial site and restore it to a valued wildlife reserve. An iron foundry and a ship-manufacturing facility occupied this site from 1907 and 1931. The ruins are their nearly 70-year old remains. Sand mining created depressions that later formed many of the 14 ponds.

The ruins overlooking Monument Pond are especially fun for kids to climb on, for enjoying the vista, and for watching wildlife.

The Ponds and Their Wildlife The preserve's 14 ponds are the largest freshwater wetland on the Island's north shore. The ponds brim with pumpkinseed, bass and Gambusia, as well as frogs and painted and snapping turtles.

The bird life is so rich because the ponds

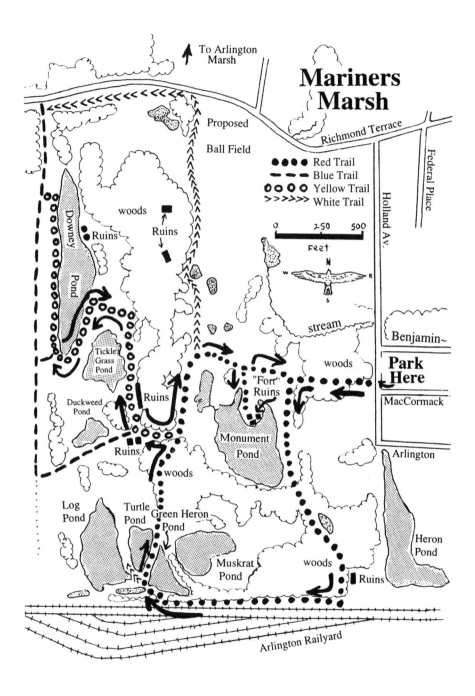

Mariners Marsh

To Arlington Marsh

Proposed Ball Field

Richmond Terrace

Federal Place

Holland Av.

● ● ● ● Red Trail
- - - Blue Trail
O O O O Yellow Trail
> > > > > White Trail

0   250   500
Feet

N
W   E
S

woods

Downey Pond

Ruins   Ruins

Tickle Grass Pond

Duckweed Pond

Ruins

Ruins

stream

woods

Benjamin

Park Here

MacCormack

"Fort" Ruins

Monument Pond

Arlington

woods

Log Pond

Turtle Pond

Green Heron Pond

Muskrat Pond

woods

Ruins

Heron Pond

Arlington Railyard

Overseeing Monument Pond from "The Fort" in Mariners Marsh

are a major feeding area for the Harbor Heron Rookery of Shooters Island, 3,000 feet away, and Prall's Island. You can see the tropical glossy ibis, great egret, and many herons, as well as the red-tail hawk and -- if you're lucky -- the unusual harrier (a marsh hawk), osprey and endangered peregrine falcon. You may see a flock of green-winged teal or Canada geese rising from a pond, or sneak a view of elusive wood ducks on Vernal Pond, or canvasbacks on Monument Pond. The eastern ponds may reveal muskrat, the work of a raccoon ... or even (yes, it's rarely seen) a deer!

The Railroad Prairie A prairie on Staten Island? Yes. It is another example of how an abandoned industrial site can naturalize into a unique habitat. The Arlington Yard railroad corridor on the south side of the preserve was always kept clear of tree and shrub growth, often by wildfires set by sparks from passing trains. This fostered growth of waving prairie grasses, golden in autumn, along the woods edge. Park lovers are now working to get the former railroad corridor from St. George to Mariners Marsh protected to create a North Shore Greenway for all to use.

How to Get There:

By Bus: Take the S48 or S98 to the corner of Holland Avenue and Arlington Place. Walk down Holland to the preserve entrance between Benjamin Place and MacCormack Place, on the opposite side.

By Car: Take S.I. Expressway to the South Avenue exit. Off the service road, turn right on South Avenue. Drive one mile to Arlington Place, make a left, then a right on Holland. Drive two blocks to preserve entrance on left (opposite Benjamin Place).

Enter the Red Trail near Benjamin Place. After passing through a lowland forest of sweet gum, gray birch, swamp white oak and prickly brier, you enter a meadow. You can identify the small sweet gum trees that grow along the rails by the deep, corky, vertical ridges in their bark. Take the *left* fork (don't go straight) on the Red Trail. After several hundred feet, look for a steep, open bank on your left. If you climb it, you get your first **view of Monument Pond**.

sweet gum

As you walk further on the trail, you re-enter a lowland forest, this time of pin oak surviving from the 1800s. Look for railroad rails, surrounded by trees that sprouted nearly 70 years ago. These rails were used to move the ships down to the Kill Van Kull's waters.

Just before you climb up to the railroad prairie path, you pass the walls of the **first ruins** on your left.

Note: Part of the rail line is being reactivated. It is not known if it will require rerouting of the Red Trail or prevent people from travelling through the prairie.

When you enter the **railroad prairie**, turn right and follow the grassland edge of the old railroad corridor. Examine the tall, rust-colored prairie grass. Also observe the short trees with large leaves that grow along the rails. These are Chinese empress trees, escaped from backyard planted trees. In mid-May, they display stunning large blossoms. In summer, seven-foot tall, woolly-leafed mullein (the perfect leaf for outdoor toilet paper) is prominent. Look carefully for the very rare American bittersweet, with its scarlet autumn berries, growing draped on the trees along the woods' edge.

After 1,000 feet of walking, turn right through a trail opening in the woods and leave the prairie. The Red Trail goes down a bank and quickly reaches an intersection. Take the wider of the two left forks (don't take any spoons though!) and go up the hill to see a fine overlook. **Log Pond** is on your left, **Turtle Pond** on your right, and **Green Heron Pond** further to the right. (Walk quietly so you'll see the wildlife.)

Turtle Pond gets covered in summer by a lime-green coating. This is not pond "scum" or "slime" but a tiny aquatic flower, in fact, the world's tiniest flowering plant, the duckweed! These minute floating dots are actually leaves with roots and even flowers, fruit and seeds. Watch for turtles on the far end of Turtle Pond (of course). Note the logs on the far end of Log Pond (of course!). These are actually old burned telephone poles, now a favorite roosting perch for wading birds.

Out in the distance are the former Procter & Gamble factory and New Jersey industry. Remember to thank Mother Nature for reclaiming this abandoned industrial site, and converting it into an island of green and blue in a sea of drab industry.

Return to the intersection and turn left on the Red Trail. About 800 feet later, turn left on the Yellow Trail. Shortly after, the Yellow Trail turns right.

As you pass the **vine-smothered ruins** on your right, you get the sense that the ghosts of a long-ago civilization may be here. Actually, if you get that sense, you may be feeling the spirit of the Indians who once lived here. A 1906 American Museum of Natural History dig here revealed this site was probably a large Indian village and burial ground!

After the ruins, the trail passes **Tickle Grass Pond**, named for the 12-foot reed (*Phragmites*) grass that lines its shores. If you break off a single long stalk at its base, the large tassels make a great tickler for unwary parents and friends!

The trail curves left and quickly reaches **Downey Pond**. Take the Yellow Trail to the open area on the opposite side and to the east shore of Downey Pond. Although Downey Pond was named after the Downey Shipyard, downy woodpeckers (our smallest) are often seen here, too. On the pond, watch for mallards and other wildlife.

Return the same way you came, on the Yellow Trail. When you reach the intersection, turn left, and left again at the Red Trail.

At a wide fork, be sure to take the right-hand Red Trail. Now look for a smaller spur trail on the right. It leads you to the **Monument Pond overlook**. This is perfect place to eat lunch (take out all of your litter!). There are three sets of **giant ruins**. Release the child in you and make sure to climb on *all* of them! From the top of the ruins, survey across Monument Pond and much of this amazing new preserve. Remember to be quiet in order to see more wildlife. In summer, you can look into the water and see sunfish.

(See the map to explore off-trail for the three ruins in other parts of the park. **Remember to watch for trenches** and to take precautions for ticks and poison ivy.)

From the "fort," return to the Red Trail and turn right. Follow it straight into the woods and you are back to the road.

To information, or to create a North Shore Greenbelt, contact:
- Mariners Marsh Conservancy
- Protectors of Pine Oak Woods   see addresses
- Friends of Clearwater   in appendix
- Audubon Society

UNEXPECTED DELIGHTS: CANOEING STATEN ISLAND'S BAYOU COUNTRY

A wild canoe adventure in a borough of New York City? Is it possible? Yes! Here is Staten Island's best-kept secret: you can weave through a watery wilderness and paddle silently through winding canyons of towering grasses. Around each bend, abundant water birds and wildlife await you. Never been canoeing? Don't know where to rent a canoe? Don't worry ... read ahead for the easy solution to that!

Distance: 4.8 miles round trip, which will take a leisurely 3 hours

Difficulty: Unloading and carrying the canoe from car to creek (and back again) requires physical exertion by two people. The rest is mostly easy flatwater paddling. However, you may need moderate effort in paddling if you are running against a stiff breeze, especially when you are going upcurrent. **Caution: avoid canoeing on windy or stormy days.**

What to Bring: Canoe guide will provide lifejackets. Bring old sneakers, sunblock lotion (summer); binoculars (if you want to see birds close-up!); plastic zip-lock bags to keep belongings dry; plastic jug of drinking water; lunch if desired; old gloves (for those prone to getting blisters from paddling).

The Easy Way to Go on a Canoe Adventure

You don't have to know how to canoe, or own a canoe, to go on this adventure! The Friends of Clearwater schedules public canoe adventures most weekends from April 15 to October 15. They provide the guides, the canoes, life jackets and the adventure spirit. Call Jim Scarcella, 718-987-6037, 7 - 9:00 pm weeknights for information or reservations (required 30 days in advance). Remember, space is limited, so plan early.

Scenic Delights:

__William T. Davis Wildlife Refuge__ Your canoe trip begins in this wild treasure: a 260-acre city park devoted just to wildlife (and wildlife lovers). Named for one of Staten Island's most famous naturalists (see accompanying article), it also offers a half mile foot trail. The Davis Refuge is New York City's *first* wildlife sanctuary, established 1928.

__The Vast Bayous of Staten Island__ The Main Creek and Fresh Kills tidal river system offers days of exploration through wild

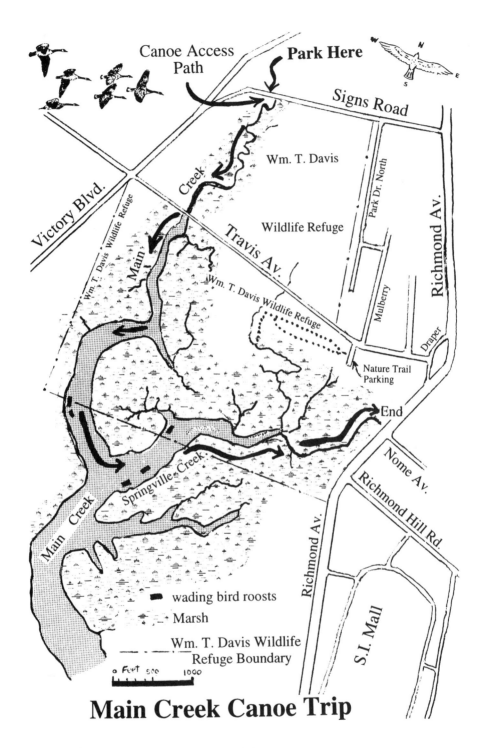

Canoe Access
Path

Park Here

Signs Road

Wm. T. Davis

Wildlife Refuge

Creek

Wm. T. Davis Wildlife Refuge

Victory Blvd.

Main Creek

Travis Av.

Wm. T. Davis Wildlife Refuge

Park Dr. North

Mulberry

Richmond Av.

Draper

Nature Trail
Parking

End

Nome Av.

Richmond Hill Rd.

Richmond Av.

Springville Creek

Main Creek

wading bird roosts

Marsh

Wm. T. Davis Wildlife
Refuge Boundary

S.I. Mall

0 Feet 500 1000

Main Creek Canoe Trip

Join a canoe adventure on the bayous of Staten Island's Fresh Kills waterways

bay and marsh country. Once considered a worthless wasteland, modern enlightened views reveal this huge wetland wilderness as a wildlife oasis that is more productive of life than almost any other natural system. Still viewed by some as a barrier to urban development, wetlands enrich urban communities by providing welcome green space and outdoor recreation, as well as air and water pollution filters and a flood control system (at no cost to taxpayers!).

The Main Creek-Fresh Kills system offers:
- 7.5 miles of canoe routes
- 1100 acres of wild marsh and a getaway for solitude
- habitat for hundreds of kinds of wildlife, some of which live their entire lives here without ever seeing a human
- historic relics of a bygone era -- wooden islands that are actually remains of salt hay barges from the 1800s that are now the roosting sites for water birds.

The Wildlife Oasis   What a thrill it is to glide in silence past walls of waving grass! Around the next bend, directly in front of you, dozens of long-necked herons, stilt-legged egrets and exotic curve-billed ibis bask in the sun. Startled, in an instant they erupt into the air. They wheel off in different directions with great wing flaps, gawky and graceful at the same time.

This is what awaits you in this wildlife paradise. Almost 120 kinds of birds have been recorded in this refuge. You can see four-foot tall great blue heron, the nearly-as-large American egret, the snowy egret with its stunningly exquisite plumage, as well as the glossy ibis (recent arrival from the tropics). Two kinds of awkward black seabirds, the cormorants, roost with the herons and gulls. Four kinds of hawk soar over the marsh, while mallards, wood ducks and many other waterfowl paddle across the bayous. Bank, barn and tree swallows flit over the water, feasting on insects. Woodcock, redwing blackbirds and dozens of other songbirds fill out the repertoire. If you are lucky, you might see large snapping turtles and muskrats. Be alert for fiddler crabs that scoot into their riverbank holes as soon as you float by.

How To Get There:

Take Staten Island Expressway to Richmond Avenue South Exit. At the junction of Richmond Avenue and Victory Blvd., turn right (west) on Victory Blvd. Drive 1.7 miles and make a left on Signs Road. (If you reach Travis Avenue, you've gone too far.) Drive 0.2 miles on Signs Road. Park at the canoe launch sign along (appropriately) Signs Road.

Carry your canoe down the short trail through the giant reed grass. It is clumsy going but soon you are at the creek. You need to walk in the shallow creek (with hard gravel bottom) to maneuver the canoe to the deeper pool of water 20 feet or so downstream.

With a little more scraping and maneuvering, you're floating! The water channel quickly deepens. You pass three partly submerged auto relicts, reminders of unfortunate urban activities that you will leave behind shortly. The creek enters a narrow meandering alley between ten-foot high walls of reed grass (*Phragmites*). You feel as if you've entered another world, one of mystery around each bend. You wonder what sight or animal could appear.

On our last visit, two huge snapping turtles engaged in sex made quite a ruckus as we rounded one bend; around the next bend appeared a half-dozen blue-green iridescent tree swallows perched only one or two feet from my face. They stared at me as much in amazement as I stared at them!

After paddling through the "canyon of reeds" for a half mile, the creek widens. Soon, you reach the low concrete Travis Avenue bridge. At high water, you may have to duck (quack, quack?) and let the canoe glide under the bridge. If needed, push yourself along with your hands on the bridge girders. **Take caution not to hit your head!**

Past the bridge, the stream widens more and more. Instead of a narrow alley-like waterway, you now enter a wide open setting of expansive marsh and water for hundreds of acres. At first, signs of civilization are barely visible. The giant earthen mound of the Fresh Kills Landfill appears like a towering but distant mesa to the south; the tall smokestacks of the Con Edison Power Plant rise 1.2 miles to the southwest. Few humans ever venture here -- that's why we call it "wilderness."

Be ready for wildlife as you paddle around each widening bend. Several islands that look like old wooden docks are likely **roosting sites** for up to dozens of wading birds and waterbirds. Have your binoculars ready! See how close you can get to them before they leap into the air. Note all the different kinds you see.

Little bays and channels will appear along the way. To keep on course, **stay in the widest channel**. Watch for the slight current to guide you. Even if you go into the wrong channel, it should quickly dead-end or become too shallow. In fact, it's lots of fun to explore the side channels.

About 20 minutes of paddling past the Travis Avenue bridge, **watch for the place where the creek divides into two wide channels**, one in front of you but bearing to the right, and another on the left. (A short while before this, you crossed the Wildlife Refuge boundary and entered the part of the creek managed by the NY Sanitation Department.)

Take the left channel. This is **Springville Creek**. You are now paddling upstream. The wide creek winds past more "wooden bird islands" and then narrows suddenly on a right-hand curve. You have re-entered the Davis Wildlife Refuge. You again become surrounded by a winding "alley" of tall marsh grass. If you paddle to its end, you will reach a concrete water control structure only yards from Richmond Avenue. The whir of out-of-sight traffic is a disconcerting contrast with the quiet wilderness behind you.

Retrace your route back to Main Creek Channel. **When you can see wide channels to the left and to the right, paddle to the right.** You will now be going upstream. Though the river current is very gentle, an ebbing tidal current might require a steady effort to make the trip upstream, especially if combined with a wind. Hug the right shore to make it easier.

When the channel narrows, the wind (if you had any) will cease. If you are returning while the tide is ebbing, you will notice the channel has narrowed. When your canoe starts scraping gravel bottom, you are a short distance from your take-out spot. Step out and drag the canoe to the path and haul your canoe out.

Status of Fresh Kills-Main Creek Wetlands

The upper part of Main Creek and its surrounding wetlands are protected as part of William T. Davis Wildlife Refuge. However, the longer stretch of Main Creek downstream, as well as Fresh Kills and the lower part of Richmond Creek, are owned by the NYC Sanitation Department. Decades of New York City's massive accumulations of garbage are now the infamous Fresh Kills Landfill, which destroyed at least half of the wetlands and wildlife of the Fresh Kills system.

In 1996, the NY State legislature passed a law mandating the closure of the Fresh Kills Landfill. The further destruction of the wetlands will end in 2002. Environmental groups want the landfills to be transformed into public open space, with the still-undisturbed wetlands transferred from the Sanitation Department to a wildlife refuge or park status.

To help protect the Fresh Kills ecosystem, contact:
- Friends of Clearwater   See Addresses
- S.I. Citizens for Clean Air   in Appendix
- Protectors of Pine Oak Woods

Credit: Harry Madden

Graceful snowy egrets and other long-legged waders flock on Main Creek

The Greenbelt

Greenbelt Features

1. Clove Lakes Park (separate park, geographically part of Greenbelt)
2. S.I. Zoo
3. Moses Folly (unused h'wy overpasses & cliffs)
4. Deer Park
5. Todt Hill Summit (412 ft.)
   Highest Pt. on Atlantic Coast, South of Maine
6. Reeds Basket Willow Swamp
7. St.Francis Woodlands
8. Central Greenbelt
9. Camp Kaufman (private lease, state owned)
10. Pouch Boy Scout Camp (private)
11. Richmond Co. Golf Course (private lease, state owned)
12. Moravian Cemetery & Vanderbilt Mausoleum (private)
13. High Rock
14. Egbertville Ravine
15. Lighthouse Hill (incl. Tibetan Museum, Lighthouse & Frank Lloyd Wright Home)
16. Amundsen Trailway (south section)
17. Mt.Moses
18. South Seaview
19. Bloodroot Valley
20. Great Swamp
21 Corsons Brook Woods
22. Willowbrook Park
23. Bucks Hollow & Heyerdahl Hill
24. Latourette Golf Course
25. Southwest Latourette Park
26. Richmond Town Historic Village
27. William T. Davis Wildlife Refuge
28. Main Creek Bayous & Canoe Trip
29. Richmond Creek
30. Childhood Home of Author

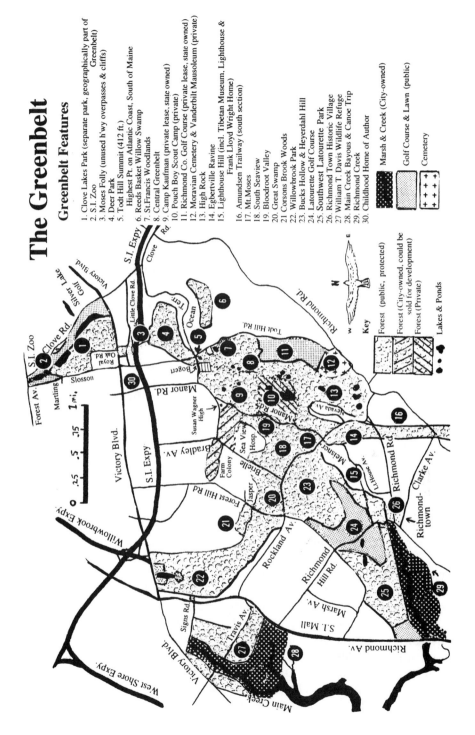

Key

- Forest (public, protected)
- Forest (City-owned, could be sold for development)
- Forest (Private)
- Lakes & Ponds
- Marsh & Creek (City-owned)
- Golf Course & Lawn (public)
- Cemetery

CLOVE LAKES PARK: WHERE THE
GREENBELT TRAIL BEGINS

Picturesque stone bridges, winding walkways, and placid ponds make this Staten Island's classic old-fashioned park. Its unique gifts are the largest living thing on Staten Island (a giant tree), and the Island's only waterfalls. This is where the amazing 35-mile long Greenbelt Trail system begins. The park's neighbor is the Staten Island Zoo, which is nationally unique as the home of one of the country's largest venomous reptile collections.

Distance: 3.5 miles round trip

Level of Difficulty: mostly easy, except a moderate climb of 120 feet on the last stretch

Things to Bring: a willingness to be humbled under Staten Island's largest tree; camera, binoculars, bird guide, bug protection, plastic bags to pick up litter. Know your poison ivy (occasional here).

Scenic Delights:
Clove Lakes Park This is Staten Island's traditional, picturesque park, similar in style to Central Park. For decades, youth groups, schools and other visitors from Manhattan and Brooklyn have traveled to Clove Lakes Park to enjoy what they thought was "the country in the city." Boy, what would they think of the Greenbelt?

The center of this pastoral setting is a string of four placid ponds: Upper and Lower Clove Lakes, Martling's Pond and Brooks Pond. "Clove" Lake was named from the Dutch word "kloven," which refers to the valley fault or crack that "cleaves" the surrounding hills. This valley was further deepened by the Ice Age Glacier of 20,000 years ago.

The 200-acre park is also graced with rustic stone arch foot bridges, winding paved walkways, and large lawns dotted with pretty landscaping. Other activities include row boating, ice skating, horseback riding, fishing, picnicking and athletic fields.

Staten Island's Only Waterfalls Three waterfalls, the Island's only ones, decorate the park. Although they are man-made, they do what all cascades do, add both serenity and sprightliness to the scenery. Between the two Clove Lakes is a smooth sheet of water over the dam. Next is a bubbling cascade over a wall of boulders. At the end of Martling's Pond is a "secret spot" where white sheets

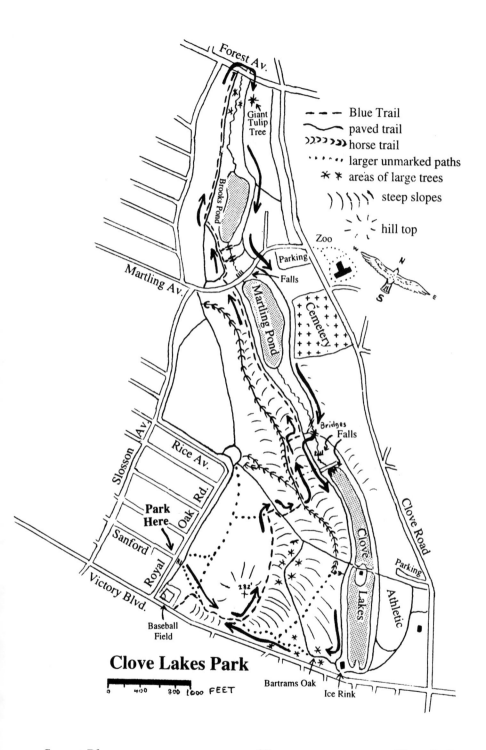

Forest Av.

Giant
Tulip
Tree

--- Blue Trail
~~~ paved trail
>>>> horse trail
····· larger unmarked paths
✳ ✶ areas of large trees
)))))) steep slopes
⟍⟋ hill top

Brooks Pond

Zoo

Parking

Falls

N
W   E
S

Martling Av.

Martling Pond

Cemetery

Bridges
Falls

Slosson Av.

Rice Av.

Oak Rd.

**Park
Here**

Sanford

Royal

Clove Road

Parking

Clove Lakes

Athletic

282'

Victory Blvd.

Baseball
Field

Bartrams Oak

Ice Rink

Clove Lakes Park

0   400   800 1000 FEET

Credit: John Prasek

Sprightly Martlings Pond Cascade at Clove Lakes Park

dance down a flight of steps under a graceful white stone arch bridge.

Giant Trees, Colorful Trees, Historic Trees Weeping willows grace the shores of the ponds. Exotic trees blossom and fruit, adding cheerful color and fragrance in spring and summer, while autumn colors brighten the spirit as the days wane. In an unmarked area of the southeast corner of the park's forest stands the **world's largest Bartram's Oak**. This rare hybrid of red and willow oaks was planted by Staten Island's beloved naturalist William T. Davis in 1888. It has different pointed and lobed shapes and the trunk is now three feet in diameter.

More than six feet in diameter and probably 300 years old -- those are the "stats" for **Staten Island's largest living thing**. It is a massive tulip tree at the northern end of the park (see page 19). The park also harbors notable groves of other towering and stately trees, as described below.

Where the Greenbelt Begins Clove Lakes Park is the northern tip of Staten Island's Greenbelt. The remarkable "belt of green" winds six miles from Forest Avenue to Richmond Town and Richmond Avenue. A major arm also extends 2.5 miles further to Willowbrook Park and William T. Davis Wildlife Refuge. Although it is geographically part of the Greenbelt, Clove Lakes Park was established in the 1920s, so it is administered separately from the new Greenbelt Park, which was created in 1984.

This is also where the Blue Trail Begins, which along with the Yellow Trail, is called the Olmsted Trailway. Formally established and blazed in 1972 by the Urban Trail Club, the trail route was named for another of Staten Island's eminent naturalists, Frederick Law Olmsted (see page 14). These are part of one of the longest continuous trail networks within a city limit anywhere in America (35 miles).

One of the Finest Small Zoos in America Little noticed outside of Staten Island is the Staten Island Zoo, which has one of the most extensive venomous reptile collections in the country. Set in an arboretum of unusual trees, it houses a lovely aquarium, a children's zoo, and newly built tropical rain forest and African savanna exhibits. Hours: 10 am - 4:45 pm daily; fee: $2 children, $3 adults, 718-442-3101.

How to Get There

By Bus: From the Ferry, take S61, S62 or S66 buses along Victory Blvd. to Royal Oak Road. Walk one block up Royal Oak Road to the intersection of Sanford Place.

By Car: Take the S.I. Expressway to the Todt Hill Road Exit. Turn north on Slosson (that's right if you came from the east, left if you came from the west). Go two blocks to Victory Blvd. Turn right on Victory, drive two blocks and turn left on Royal Oak Road. In one block, park at the intersection of Sanford Place.

Walk toward the woods and up the slate rock steps. Cross the paved bikeway and head straight to the wide path that heads into the woods. The wide path passes one side path and dips down a long hill over wood chips. Now watch for blue blazes on some trees. Part way downhill, *carefully watch for a second left*, a small foot trail on the left, with a blue blaze on a tree. Turn here.

The narrow Blue Trail crosses along the side of Clove Lakes Hill, passing through dry woods of red, black, white and chestnut oak, and sassafras and hickory. Ignore six or so cross-paths. Watch for the blue blazes where the path finally makes a right downhill. Moments later, it "hits" (not too hard, I hope!) a paved path. Turn right and, in about a hundred feet, *very carefully watch* for where the Blue Trail cuts off to the left. As it descends, look for the scattered evergreen trees in the woods. These are hemlock trees, at their southernmost location on the U.S. coast.

red oak

sassafras

hemlock tree

Shortly after, the Blue Trail reaches a horse path and joins it. Just ahead, it follows its right fork. Again, *carefully watch for the blue blazes* as they separate from the horse path and descend.

You are now on the paved walkway. On the other side, notice two picturesque red wooden bridges. Turn left on the walkway. Enjoy the quiet creek, the exotic landscape trees and the people: strolling, jogging, skating, picnicking, smooching, fishing, whatever soothes the soul! The sparkling placid waters of **Martling's Pond** (named for a S.I. member of the 1820s state infantry) now become a welcome addition to your scenery.

When you reach Martling Avenue, go left along the sidewalk *watching carefully for a double blaze* on a tree that tells you to cross the street to a single blaze on a tree on the other side. Cross the street.

But before you continue on the Blue Trail, take a little detour to a delightful treat. Turn right and walk to the graceful stone bridge across the pond's outlet. Look to your left and straight down, where you'll see a cascade. Here's how to get to the "secret spot."

At the end of the bridge, just as the wooden fence ends, walk only ten feet and push your way into the thick vegetation on your left. Carefully climb down the steep bank and you'll emerge in the "secret spot." Here is a 25-foot series of **silky cascade** steps emptying out of the bridge tunnel and into a tranquil pool. Sit awhile and let the swoosh of white noise soothe the stress of city life. If you go in July, you can eat an unlimited supply of luscious mulberries (which look like blackberries) from overhanging branches.

Return to the Blue Trail. It steeply descends to a paved path, passing two scenic foot bridges on your right (one wooden, one white stone). Check them out but then return to the Blue Trail, which soon bears left on the paved path. A marsh of towering reed grasses and then **Brooks Pond** appears to your right. Merge with a wider walkway. Soon, you parallel a pretty brook. Note the huge boulders in it. This stretch of stream also offers the best warbler watching on S.I. in spring. Pass many impressive tulip trees and oaks, about 150 to 200 years old. When you reach Forest Avenue, you are now at the northern beginning of the Greenbelt and its trail system. The stream flows another 0.8 mile to the salty Kill Van Kull through old urban neighborhoods and an industrial areas.

Turn right on Forest Avenue and right again on the first paved path. Two hundred feet down the path, watch for the **Champion tulip tree** to your left in the field. This is the largest living thing on Staten Island! Make sure to walk up to it, and also put your hand on it -- to really appreciate how truly massive it is. It probably was a seedling in Staten Island's original primeval forest around 1700. See how many people or arm spreads it takes to reach around the tree. Watch for poison ivy.

Return to the paved path. Notice several other large tulip trees and oaks nearby. When the paved path reaches a fork, take the narrower one. Enjoy glistening **Brooks Pond** and all the people lounging around it during warmer months. When you reach any fork (not spoon or knife though!), always take the left one. Do not cross a foot bridge, or you will leave the route described here.

Arrive at Martling Avenue. (If you walk a couple of blocks to your left, you will arrive at the **Staten Island Zoo**. Visit it if you can! You can also buy snacks and make a pit stop.)

Cross Martling Avenue and continue walking the path along the pond. Watch for waterbirds, especially honking Canada geese, mallard, graceful great egret, cackling ringed-bill and herring gulls, maybe even a kingfisher.

When you cross a pretty wooden footbridge, you may recognize it -- you passed it when you exited the woods earlier. Bear left and follow the wide paved path along the edge of the stream.

Look on your left for the **waterfall** and walk up to it. Enjoy it and the rustic stone bridge. While walking further along the paved walkway, watch boaters and anglers on **Clove Lake**. On the island in the lake, you can "get romantic the old-fashioned way" and rent a row boat.

The wide walkway comes to the fence of the ice rink. When the ice rink ends just before Victory Blvd., take the right fork back into the woods. It parallels Victory Blvd. and ascends a long hill, passing more impressive oaks and tulip trees. (The unmarked **World Champion Bartram's oak** is off to your right.) *When the paved path forks to the right, take the unpaved left fork.* As a kid, this was the author's favorite sledding hill.

When you reach the top of the hill, you have just made a 120-foot climb. Moments later, you emerge at Royal Oak Road.

For information, and to help protect the Greenbelt, contact:
- Protectors of Pine Oak Woods
- Staten Island Zoo   see addresses
- Urban Trail Club (to help blaze trails)   in appendix
- NY City Dept. of Parks & Recreation

HOW TO CLIMB THE HIGHEST POINT ON THE ATLANTIC SEABOARD: TODT HILL

Climb the highest hill on the U.S. Atlantic Seaboard, south of Maine. Walk across Moses' Folly, a monument to the highway project that would have destroyed the Greenbelt. Observe the unique green serpentine rock that makes up Staten Island's backbone, a rock formed when continents collided long, long ago.

Distance: 2.4 mile round trip.

Level of Difficulty: strenuous but short climb in the beginning; later, a moderate but longer climb. Total climb: 212 feet.

Things to Bring: Sturdy hiking shoes, water, plastic bags to pick up litter, bug protection. Know your poison ivy (occasional here).

Scenic Delights:

Highest Point on Atlantic Seaboard You may have known that Staten Island is hilly, but it is truly the highest point on the U.S. Atlantic Coast from southern Maine to the tip of Florida. That highest point (412 feet above sea level) is on Todt Hill, 600 feet south of the intersection of Ocean Terrace and Todt Hill Road. With an ascent of 212 feet, this hike makes it clear you are climbing to the highest point! (Rumors that the Fresh Kills Landfill became the highest point just aren't true; the landfill will reach 175 feet above sea level before it is closed in 2002.)

Staten Island's Unique Serpentine Backbone The hilly backbone of Staten Island is made of a rather rare rock called serpentine. Serpentine is a light green, soft, smooth rock related to soapstone and talc. It is found in quantity in few places in the world, the nearest being Pennsylvania and Quebec. It is dramatically exposed in the 70-foot cliffs overlooking the Staten Island Expressway near the Todt Hill Road Exit. Outcroppings (surface exposures) of serpentine are also seen at numerous places from Clove Lakes Park to Richmond Town.

What makes it even more fascinating is that it is actually the "seam" between the ancient continents of North America and Africa when they very slowly collided 230 million years ago, before the Age of Dinosaurs. That gradual crunching caused by continental drift (slow movement of continental plates due to flowing of underground molten rock deep below) pushed up the Appalachian mountains. The edge of intense contact and pressure formed the unique

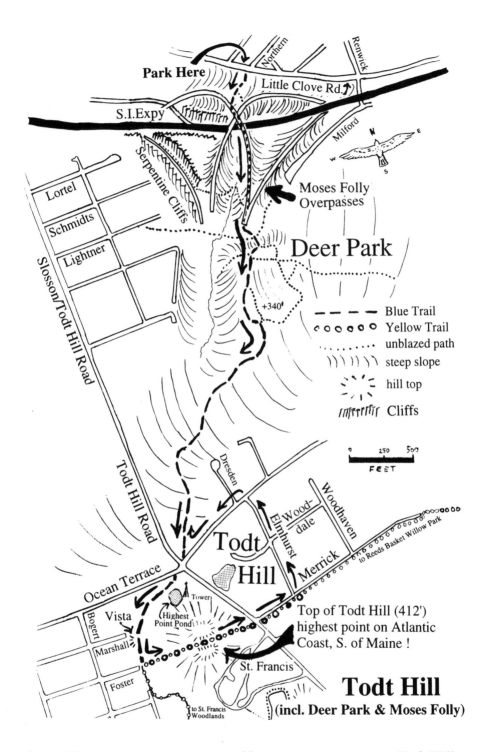

Park Here

Northern

Renwick

Little Clove Rd.

S.I.Expy

Milford

N
E
W
S

Moses Folly
Overpasses

Lortel

Schmidts

Lightner

Serpentine Cliffs

Deer Park

+340'

Slosson/Todt Hill Road

Todt Hill Road

- - - - Blue Trail
○○○○○○ Yellow Trail
············· unblazed path
))))))) steep slope
☀ hill top
⌐⌐⌐⌐⌐⌐ Cliffs

0   250   500

FEET

Dresden

Wood-dale

Woodhaven

Elmhurst

to Reeds Basket Willow Park

Todt
Hill

Merrick

Ocean Terrace

Tower

Vista

(Highest
Point Pond)

Bogert

Top of Todt Hill (412')
highest point on Atlantic
Coast, S. of Maine !

Marshall

St. Francis

Foster

to St. Francis
Woodlands

Todt Hill
(incl. Deer Park & Moses Folly)

serpentine seen in the Metro Area only on Staten Island.

Moses' Folly The abandoned highway overpasses and "cloverleaf" just east of the Todt Hill Exit of S.I. Expressway have been there since 1964. That is when Staten Island's environ mental and save-the-Greenbelt movement was born. This happened because these overpasses were to lead to *con*struction of the Richmond Parkway, which would have led to *de*struction of the very Greenbelt showcased in this book. The highway was championed by Robert F. Moses, the dynamic and very often dictatorial public official who fathered many other public

70-foot green serpentine cliffs at foot of Todt Hill

works projects throughout the state, some beneficial, some not. Along with the great success in protecting High Rock (see p.66), the 25-year battle to halt the Richmond Parkway was the other legendary environmental success. Moses' Folly memorializes his role in pushing an unnecessary project that would have forever destroyed Staten Island's unique rural character and scenic and natural heritage. Moses' Folly reminds us of the thoughtless mega-plans of a few power brokers and is a tribute to the dedication and long persistence of caring and committed ordinary citizens who love Staten Island.

Deer Park Deer Park is the 60-acre north-facing slope of Todt Hill. The hill's high vantage point did not go unnoticed by the British, who used it as a look-out post during the Revolutionary War.

How to Get There

By Bus: Take Victory Blvd. buses such as the S61, 62, 66, or 67 to Renwick Ave. (a side street of Victory Blvd. opposite Clove Lakes Park). Walk a block down Renwick to Northern Blvd.; take a right on Northern to Little Clove Road.

By Car: From the Verrazano Bridge, take the S.I. Expressway to Richmond Road Exit. Take the Service Road, cross Clove Road and continue straight; it will become Little Clove Road.

From the west, take S.I. Expressway to Clove Road/Richmond Road Exit. Take the Service Road to Clove Road. Turn left on Clove Road, cross over the Expressway and immediately make a left on the service road, which becomes Little Clove Road.

Drive 0.5 mi. on Little Clove Rd. to Northern Blvd. on your right. Park here.

To find the trailhead from where Little Clove Road meets Northern Blvd., walk 100 feet uphill along Little Clove Road. Look for the break in the fence on the highway side of the road. That is the Blue Trail.

Your climb to the highest point on the Atlantic seaboard begins immediately -- a very steep 50-foot ascent. On the way uphill, take the fork on the right. At the top, you are on **Moses' Folly**. Turn left on the never-used ramp across the Expressway. In the distance, the **Verrazano Bridge** (three miles away) is framed by **Grymes Hill** (370 feet elev.) on the left, **Emerson Hill** (340 feet elev.) on the right. Look at the 70-foot cliffs along the highway -- these are the continental seam of serpentine described above. The Blue Trail follows the old highway ramp toward the forested **Todt Hill** ahead of you.

(At the point where a second ramp joins *from the left*, look for a side path *to the right*, down the side of the steep bank. If you want a detour to visit the impressive **green serpentine cliffs**, take this side path down. It crosses a ravine (and a junked vehicle), then ascends to another old ramp. Cross to the ramp's other side, walk across a field and you enter the "canyon" between the impressive cliffs. Rare minerals and crystals were found here when this was blasted during the Expressway's construction in 1963. Return the way you came.)

Where the ramp ends and the woods begin, follow the Blue Trail up the hill through dry woods of white, black and chestnut oak. Watch for the heavily scented pinxter azalea in spring and highbush blueberry fruiting in mid-summer. You cross another foot path, but always stay on the Blue Trail (watch carefully for those blazes!). Stay straight and always head uphill.

chestnut oak

pinxter azalea

Note the green rock exposed along the trail. Find a fresh piece of serpentine and feel its smoothness. You quickly come to a wide prairie clearing with other foot paths. Bear left uphill, always following the blue blazes. At the next fork, bear right on the Blue

Trail. The footway begins to level off. Pass another foot path, turn right and then head downhill a short distance.

Finally, the Blue Trail reaches the junction of Ocean Terrace and Todt Hill Road, 0.5 mile and 190 feet higher than you began. **Caution: this is a very dangerous junction !** Cross the intersection in the following way. First cross Todt Hill Road; then walk along Ocean Terrace about 50 feet to cross it (**take extreme caution!**). On the other side, look for where the trail cuts into the woods and enter it.

You are now walking through woods near the top of Todt Hill. Hidden in the woods to the left is **Highest Point Pond**, the highest elevation pond on the Atlantic Seaboard, south of Maine. After a few minutes, look on the right to where a field comes close to the trail. Walk 20 feet out to the field to see a **vista** across New Jersey. On a clear day, the Watchung Range is visible 16 miles away. Although you are slightly lower than the highest point, this is the only trail-side vista near the summit because forest obscures the view at the highest point.

When the Blue Trail meets the Yellow Trail at a gate, head left around the gate and follow the Yellow Trail This woods "road" (actually a pipeline right-of-way) climbs a gentle rise, 450 feet from where you left the Blue Trail. Although it is relatively flat on top, you are now at **Todt Hill's summit: the highest point on the U.S. Atlantic Seaboard** (south of Maine's Camden Hills and Acadia Park).

Here's how Todt Hill may have gotten its name When someone in the congregation of the old Moravian Church died, the funeral wagon had to take the body up steep Todt Hill to the Moravian Cemetery on the other side. "Todt" Hill is Old Dutch for "Death" Hill.

When the Yellow Trail arrives at Todt Hill Road, cross it to Merrick Street (**Caution: very dangerous road with blind curves!**). Walk on Merrick and make a left on Elmhurst. Appreciate the **beautiful homes** and elegant landscaping. When you reach Ocean Terrace, turn left until you reach Todt Hill Road intersection (**again, take extreme caution and move away from traffic when cars drive by!**). At the corner of the intersection, turn right onto the Blue Trail and return down the same trail you climbed.

The trail descends, then climbs again to a ridge. Ignore unmarked foot paths and stay on the Blue Trail all the way down the hill. Follow the Blue Trail out of the woods and onto Moses' Folly. **Immediately after crossing the overpass bridge**, turn right and down the steep slope back to Little Clove Road.

For information or to join park protection efforts:
- Protectors of Pine Oak Woods
- Urban Trail Club (to help trail blaze)
- Greenbelt Park

white oak

see addresses in appendix

THE MEDITATION PLACE: ST. FRANCIS WOODLANDS
AND THE PICTURE POSTCARD VISTA

Visit the splendid St. Francis Woodlands, open for the first time to the public. Meditate in a secluded valley of majestic trees, or by a pretty and previously private pond. Mellow out at a picture-perfect vista overlooking an emerald green landscape with far away views out to 14 miles.

Distance: 1.3 mile loop
Level of Difficulty: easy, with short stretches of moderate slopes
Things to Bring: an appreciation of tranquillity or even reverence; camera, binoculars, tree and flower guides, plastic bags to pick up litter, bug protection. Know your poison ivy.

Scenic Delights:
St. Francis Seminary and Woodlands For decades, St. Francis Woodlands was the secret jewel of the Greenbelt: secluded, privately owned and essentially off-limits to the public. This book is the first to describe this special place for public visitation. Since the 1960s, environmentalists feared that one day the Franciscans would want to sell it to developers and its 23 acres of splendid woodlands, pond and picturesque buildings could be lost. That day seemed to arrive in 1995 when the "jewel of the island" went up for sale. Greenbelt lovers and state and city officials quickly began negotiations and tried to commit state environmental bond act funds for its acquisition. After a time of seat-of-your-pants suspense, success was finally realized by early 1998. St. Francis is now secure!

Because it has been undisturbed for so long, the St. Francis Woodlands contain a superb grove of towering tulip trees, sweet gum and oak trees. Most of the Greenbelt's forest was cut by the late 1800s. It is believed that this protected stand was one of the groves from which the future forest spread to regenerate today's forest.

The Cropsey Overlook and Vista The "Picture Post Card Vista" -- this is what the Cropsey Overlook offers. Along with Mt. Moses, this is the finest viewpoint from the Greenbelt. It is named for 19th century painter Jasper Cropsey whose painting (see Foreword, p. *x*) of this sweeping vista is now housed in the S.I. Institute of Arts & Sciences. The overlook is a rustic and picturesque wooden observation deck where the edge of the Greenbelt forest meets the north corner of the Richmond County Golf Course.

How to Get There:
By Bus: Take the S54 south on Manor Road to Ocean Terrace. Walk up

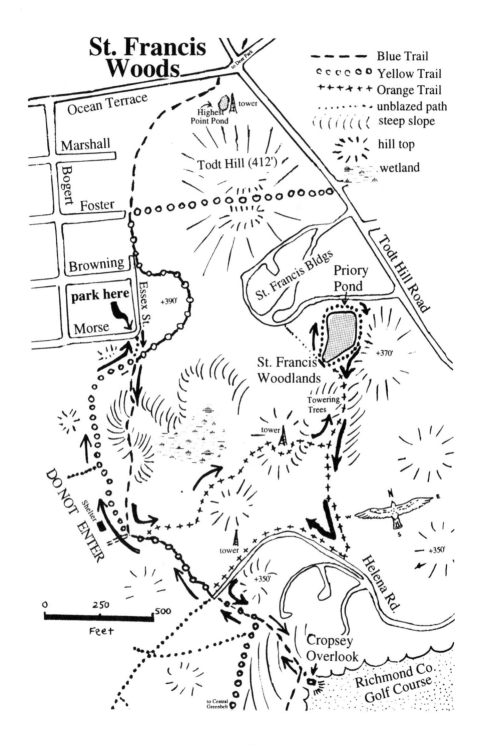

St. Francis Woods

Legend:
- – – – – Blue Trail
- ℮℮℮℮℮℮ Yellow Trail
- +++++++ Orange Trail
- ·········· unblazed path
- (((((((steep slope
- hill top
- wetland

Ocean Terrace

Marshall

Bogert

Foster

Browning

park here

Morse

Essex St.

Highest Point Pond

tower

Todt Hill (412')

+390'

DO NOT ENTER

Shelter

St. Francis Bldgs

Priory Pond

St. Francis Woodlands

Towering Trees

+370'

Todt Hill Road

tower

tower

tower

+350'

+350'

Helena Rd.

N
E
W
S

+350'

Cropsey Overlook

Richmond Co. Golf Course

to Central Greenbelt

0   250   500
Feet

to Deer Park

The "Picture Postcard Vista" at Cropsey Overlook (NJ Highlands in distance)

Ocean Terrace, make a right on Peru Street, turn left on Morse and go to the end.

By Car: From the east, take S.I. Expressway to Todt Hill Road-Slosson Avenue Exit. Cross Slosson and follow the service road to the next light. Turn left on Manor Road. If coming from the west, take the Expressway to Bradley Avenue Exit. Cross Bradley and follow the service road to the second light. Turn right on Manor Road. At Ocean Terrace, turn left up the steep hill. Make a right on Peru St. part way up the hill, then a left on Morse St. Drive to its end. Park where it meets Essex St.

At the corner of Morse and Essex, a foot path begins at the big black and white sign "No Motorized Vehicles Please." Fifty feet after entering the footpath, the Yellow and Blue combined Trails enter from your left. The Yellow Trail goes to the right -- you will return this way. *Walk straight ahead on the Blue Trail.*

Enjoy the walk up and down little rolling hills of glacial moraine, deposits of gravel and soil dropped by the Ice Age glacier 15,000 years ago. Stately, shady black, red and white oaks, sweet gum, tulip trees and beech surround you.

After crossing a hollow, you enter a cleared area where a gravel road from Camp Kaufman curves into a shelter to your right. *Stay away; it is private!* Near where the trail veers left, observe the radio towers through the trees on the left.

Shortly after the camp shelter clearing, watch for the Orange Trail blazes on your left. Take the Orange Trail through attractive woods, cross a brook ravine, and ascend to the clearing around a radio tower (for the College of Staten Island's radio station WSIA). Cross to the opposite side of the tower and re-enter the woods.

Watch for a trail junction where the Orange Trail goes both ways. You take the left turn (you will return to this point later).

Cross a brook. You are now in a splendidly beautiful, secluded valley with towering trees. You are walking through the **St. Francis Woodlands** (just purchased from the former Seminary), virtually off-limits to the public since the early 1900s. Stop momentarily and feel the solitude and tranquillity of this special valley. It is not surprising that this is the woods of a long-time religious retreat.

The Orange Trail ascends a hill and soon reaches the mirror-like **Priory Pond**, covered with green duckweed in summer. This is another place to sit and meditate, only 650 feet from the highest point on the U.S. Atlantic Seaboard, south of Maine (see p. 46). Cross the concrete dam, immediately turn right on the unmarked trail and walk around the shore of the pond, enjoying the pretty scene. Loop around the pond. Return on the Orange Trail the way you came.

After re-crossing the brook at the bottom of the wooded valley, *watch carefully for the trail junction. You proceed left, NOT on the right fork.* This part of the Orange Trail takes you to the lower valley and comes out onto Helena Road. Turn right and follow the road. Just before it ends, walk along the left side to avoid a muddy area. The end of the road meets the Blue and Yellow Trail.

Turn left on the blue-blazed gravel road and walk until you reach the road's end at the **Cropsey Vista** observation deck. **Note:** private homes are located just inside the woods to the left. **Show respect and conduct yourself quietly. Also, walking on the golf course is off-limits.** Please remove any litter you find!

Savor the exquisite **vista**. This is *the* place to mellow out and re-energize yourself! Undulating downward is the classical, pastoral landscape of the golf course, with New Dorp, Great Kills Park and Lower New York Bay beyond it. On a clear day, New Jersey's Atlantic Highlands and Sandy Hook can be seen, 14 miles away. The vista is especially beautiful in May's spring green colors and flowering trees, and in autumn's golden and scarlet foliage.

Return the way you came. Pass the end of Helena Road and continue on the Blue and Yellow Trail. When you enter the clearing where the camp shelter is, watch for the fork where the Blue Trail bears right and the *Yellow Trail continues ahead, nearer to the shelter. Take the Yellow Trail fork* to return a different way. Follow the Yellow Trail till it meets the Blue Trail later.

Now watch carefully: at the junction where the Yellow Trail rejoins with the Blue Trail, see the *short unblazed path on your left.* Follow this unblazed path up the hill and you return to Morse Street.

For information, or to help protect the Greenbelt, contact:
- Protectors of Pine Oak Woods   see addresses
- Urban Trail Club (to help blaze trails)   in appendix

WEAVING YOUR WAY THROUGH WILLOWBROOK

Wind your way through a stately forest. Eat lunch at the ruins of a giant stone chimney and fireplace in the middle of the woods. Walk through the Willowbrook Parkway right-of-way, once planned to become an expressway, now a safe and peaceful forest for wildlife and walkers.

Distance: 3.5 mile round trip

Level of Difficulty: easy

Things to Bring: bug protection (this lowland woods is more likely to be buggier than most of the Greenbelt); plastic bags to pick up litter, binoculars, bird and tree guides. Know your poison ivy (common here).

Scenic Delights:
Stately Lowland Forest One section of Willowbrook's forest contains large and stately tulip trees that are a delight to stroll under. This is a large forest; you have little idea how dense and close the development and commercial strips are.

Most of Staten Island's sizable stands of forest are hilly. That is because woods on flat ground were cleared and developed first. Willowbrook has what could be the island's largest stand of mature flatland forest. Because it is flat, it has poor drainage and has areas of standing water through winter and spring.

A little history trivia: Willowbrook is remembered in the history books as the "Great Swamp" that hid American soldiers during the Revolutionary War.

The Giant Stone Chimney How curious it is to find a 20-foot tall stone chimney and fireplace in the middle of the woods. Before its 161 acres became a park long ago, this area contained meadows, farmland and homesteads. The fireplace is what remains of a home that was probably built in the 1800s. Look at the hearth stones. They are made of rock that does not come from Staten Island, but were transported here by the Ice Age glaciers 15,000 years ago.

The White Trail and the Willowbrook "Parkway" The White Trail runs through Willowbrook and also extends through the right-of-way of the former Willowbrook Parkway. Both the Richmond and Willowbrook Parkways would have destroyed most of the Greenbelt, including Willowbrook Park. As you walk the White Trail, remember you are along an undeveloped highway corridor that still is officially "on the books." Only grass-roots pressure

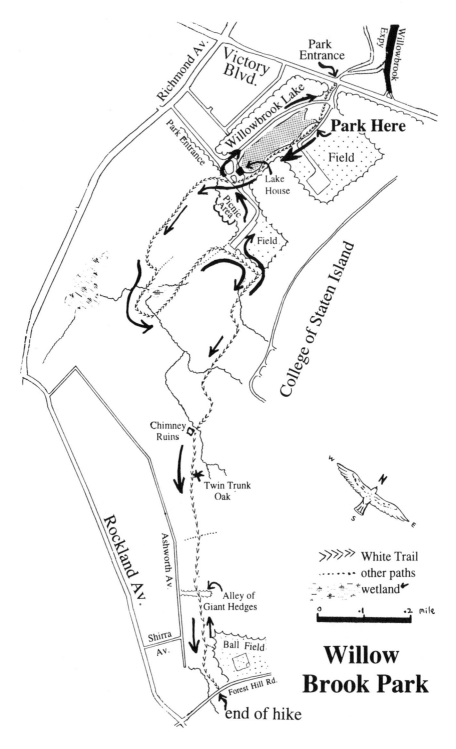

Park
Entrance

Willowbrook
Expy

Victory
Blvd.

Richmond Av.

Willowbrook Lake

Park Here

Park Entrance

Field

Lake
House

Picnic
Area

Field

College of Staten Island

Chimney
Ruins

Twin Trunk
Oak

Rockland Av.

Ashworth Av.

N

W   E

S

>>>>> White Trail
.... other paths
─── ⁔ wetland

0   .1   .2   mile

Alley of
Giant Hedges

Shirra
Av.

Ball Field

Forest Hill Rd.

end of hike

Willow
Brook Park

has prevented it from being built.

How to Get There:

By Bus: Take the S62 to Willowbrook Park entrance off Victory Blvd.

By Car: Going west, take S.I. Expressway to Exit at Victory Blvd. Turn left at the end of the exit onto Victory Blvd. After the College of Staten Island, make a left into the Willowbrook Park entrance. Park at the first parking lot near Willowbrook Pond.

The White Trail begins on the lake side of the parking lot. Look for white blazes ontrees and follow the paved path along the shore of the pond. If you followed the White Trail *all* the way to its end, you would walk

The Great Stone Chimney deep in Willowbrook Park

four miles and end up at Richmond Road. Look across the ball fields to your left to see buildings of the new College of Staten Island above the trees.

Part way along the pond, the road veers left, but the trail goes straight. Follow it along the shore into woods, *always following the white blazes.* Note: it can be muddy in spring or after heavy rains. The pond is a good place to watch for migrating ducks and geese.

When you reach the boathouse at the other end of the pond, look across the parking lot (ahead and to the right) for a playground. Walk to it and carefully look for white blazes on trees at the edge of the woods.

You enter attractive woods of tulip trees, red oak, beech and red maple. Spring brings a carpet of wildflowers. The trail joins with an unmarked path. Bear right; always follow white blazes. As the trail curves left, enjoy the stately tulip trees.

At the next fork (why not a fork and a spoon?), make sure to take the White Trail as it makes a left turn. The trail curves to the right, behind the archery field. Don't take the path to the left which returns to the pond.

You have now entered the most impressive part of the forest. Put your hand on the **large tulip trees** to get a real feel for their size.

The trail makes a right turn and takes you into the wilder woods of pin oak and sweet gum. It crosses one brook and then a larger brook. Here are the **giant stone chimney** remains of a former settler home. Look at the boulders -- they are made of non-native rock carried from 50 to 100 miles north by the Ice Age glaciers.

As you continue on the White Trail, you pass a hollow twin-trunked giant red oak. Soon the woods become younger. At the next trail intersection, keep going straight, following the White Trail.

Now you enter an odd, hard-to-describe feature. Look for the white blaze as the trail enters a "**giant hedge alleyway**" formed by an abandoned driveway between high walls of very old planted hedge. This privet hedge, the most giant I have ever seen, was once neat and trimmed, when it was the entrance to a home (demolished in the 1950s for the would-be Willowbrook Parkway).

After the hedge "alley," the woods are very young and scrubby. It was someone's yard or meadow only 30 to 40 years ago. Watch for thorny rose branches, which are not pleasant to the skin.

Shortly after, you pass a brook on the right, then you pass behind a Little League field and finally reach Forest Hill Road. This is the end of this suggested hike. As of this writing, the White Trail follows Forest Hill Road to Rockland Avenue and then re-enters the woods into Latourette park and Heyerdahl Hill (see p.84). However, there are plans to extend the White Trail into the woods across Forest Hill Road to avoid walking along dangerous roads.

To return, just follow the White Trail back, always watching carefully for the white blazes. When you pass the stone chimney and cross two brooks, you are nearing the park's ball fields. As you enter the grove of large trees, watch for an unblazed but wide foot path to your right. This is the short-cut back, cutting off a half mile. Take this right-hand foot path and quickly reach the end of a parking lot and driveway next to an archery field. Follow the driveway to the pond. *Pass the pond* and turn right onto a paved bike path that parallels the other side of Willowbrook Pond. When it meets the entrance road on the other end, your parking lot is nearby.

For information, or to help protect the park, contact:
- Protectors of Pine Oak Woods
- Urban Trail Club (to help blaze trails)   see addresses
- NY City Dept. of Parks & Recreation   in appendix

CORSON'S BROOK WOODS: ANCIENT FOREST AND THE "IMPRISONED" MERRY-GO-ROUND

Marvel at one of the most ancient forest groves in New York City. Wander your way along a clean clear brook. Chuckle at a bizarre "imprisoned" children's merry-go-round. Tour the Island's newest college campus -- the attractive College of Staten Island.

Distance: 0.8 mile round trip

Level of Difficulty: easy, but extra effort is needed to travel through woods without a trail

Things to Bring: a sense of beauty and a sense of humor; bug protection, camera, tree and flower guides, plastic bags to pick up litter. Know your poison ivy (occasional here).

Scenic Delights:

Corson's Brook Woods One of the three oldest woodlands in Staten Island, it is a majestic stand of oak and tulip trees that attain massive size and are more than 150 years old. The woods were named after Cornelius Corson, who was Staten Island's first police captain (1685). The forest survived cutting and destruction by being part of the old Halloran VA Hospital, followed by the Willowbrook Hospital grounds. The forest just grew there, unnoticed, undisturbed. After the Willowbrook Hospital was dismantled, however, the state planned to cut down the 21-acre forest for a development, even though less unique sites were available very close by. After they bulldozed three acres, park supporters mounted a grassroots campaign and court battle to stop it (the author is proud to have been part of it). It took an appeal to Governor Cuomo to stop it. The future of Corson's Brook Woods has still never been guaranteed.

The "Imprisoned" Merry-Go-Round What an off-beat thing to feature in a book! But the author just couldn't help it. You can't hold back your chuckles at such an absurd sight: an aged wood and iron children's merry-go-round "imprisoned" by small trees. A dozen trunks up to six inches thick encircle the entire structure and grow up through and between every bar and slat of this playground equipment. It was abandoned 30 or so years ago when this section of the notorious Willowbrook Hospital for retarded and disabled children was shut down. Try sitting on the turning platform. You can't budge it. I felt a sense of comical absurdity at the craziness of it -- and a touch of sadness when I thought of the long-ago disabled children who once played on it.

The College of Staten Island When the Willowbrook insti-

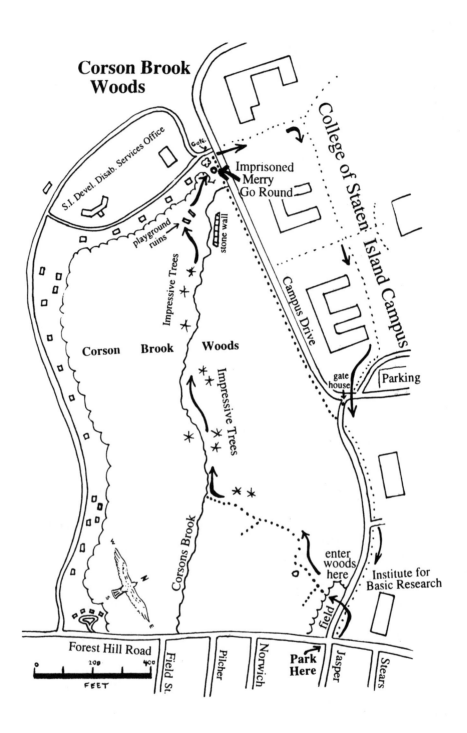

Corson Brook Woods

College of Staten Island Campus

S.I. Devel. Disab. Services Office

Gate

Imprisoned
Merry
Go Round

playground
ruins

stone wall

Impressive Trees

Corson   Brook   Woods

Impressive Trees

Campus Drive

Parking

gate
house

Corsons Brook

enter
woods
here

Institute for
Basic Research

field

Forest Hill Road

Field St.

Picher

Norwich

**Park
Here**

Jasper

Stears

0   200   400

FEET

tution was completely shut down in 1987, a vast campus of 204 acres was left without a use. After many years of uncertainty, a wise decision was made to convert it into the College of S.I. campus (called "adaptive re-use"). Although it needs more landscaping, the campus and its buildings are attractive and deserve a tour.

How to Get There:

By Bus: Take the S61 down Forest Hill Road. Get off at Jasper Street.

By Car: Going west on the S.I. Expressway, exit at Bradley Avenue; follow the service road parallel to the expressway for 0.6 mile till you reach Woolley Avenue. Make a left on Woolley, which becomes Forest Hill Road. In about half a mile, make a left on Jasper Street. Park here.

From Jasper Street, walk across Forest Hill Road to the entrance road of College of S.I. Walk down the left side of the campus road, making sure to count metal lamp posts. *At the fifth metal post*, sight the trail opening at the edge of the woods across the meadow (which is the former woods bulldozed by the state).

As you enter the foot path, walk straight ahead (don't take side paths). In summer, the foot path may be somewhat narrow with ingrown branches. As you near Corson's Brook, the trees will get more mature and impressive. When you reach the brook, the foot path ends. No problem -- you can reach the best part without a trail. Turn right, cross the brook and follow along the stream through the woods. Enjoy the fact that the brook is remarkably clean.

For the next 800 feet, admire the majestic beech, red and black oak, and tulip trees, some more than 150 years old. This is not a place to rush, nor is there a place you have to get to -- you're already "here" in a small grove of **primeval forest**.

beech

Try to find the largest trees on either side of the brook. One tulip tree is nearly four feet in diameter. Observe that its first bough starts 65 feet up, a sign that it started growing in a mature forest because it could only branch when it reached adequate light at that height. Notice also the large glacial boulders ("erratics"), another sign that the area was never farmed in the Dutch Colonial era.

You may notice sugar maple grows here, the only other place in Staten Island besides Bloodroot Valley. Look for edible wild garlic. Because the area has been undisturbed for more than a century, there are many uncommon plants, such as the giant Goldies fern, zigzag goldenrod, *Allium tricoccum* and others.

sugar maple

As you walk downstream, you will sight old red brick walls on the other side of the stream. Bear left (did you say there's a *bear* on the left?) until you're 50 feet away from the stream. This way you will avoid walking through a thorny blackberry patch. You will also

pass by parts of a play-
ground abandoned 30 or
so years ago when the
infamous Willowbrook
School was closed.

As soon as you emerge
on to a lawn, walk to
your right. Follow the
edge of the woods until
you reach the
**"imprisoned merry-go-
round"** surrounded by
small trees. (**Note:** you
are on institutional pro-
perty, not park land --
**respect it by staying
away from buildings.**)
Chuckle at how ridic-
ulous this thing is.
Examine how the trees
grew so neatly through
its bars. Try to imagine
what it will look like 30
more years from now
when the trees have
doubled in size! Try to

Tree hugger Dick Buegler, Corson's Brook Woods

imagine when the very last disabled children spun it around.

As soon as you are ready to move on, leave directly through
the nearby entrance gate. Across the road, you enter the beautiful
campus of the College of Staten Island. This attractive new college
was built in 1992 on the site of the former Willowbrook School.
Walk across the campus perimeter road and head between the two
buildings in front of you (science building on your left, psychology
building on your right). To get back to Forest Hill Road, turn right
after you pass the buildings. The large domed building on your left
is the library and the next on your right is the nursing building.

After the nursing building, bear *right* (why aren't the bears
on the left?) and you reach the perimeter drive. Walk to the entrance
station and ask for a map of the campus if you want to tour it further
-- it's huge! To return, walk back out the entrance drive.

For information, or to help protect the Woods, contact:
- Protectors of Pine Oak Woods   see addresses
- Greenbelt Park   in appendix

"I CAN'T BELIEVE THIS IS NEW YORK CITY!"
THE CENTRAL GREENBELT

You will be amazed that you are really in New York City when you hike this magnificent hill and lake scenery. Discover the wildest and most remote spot in the five boroughs. Tour six lakes and ponds, each with its own unique character. Walk beneath ancient trees in a woodland and wetland haven for wildlife.

Distance: 2.6 mile round loop

Level of Difficulty: easy to moderate, except several short but steep slopes

Things to Bring: an appreciation of wildness; camera, binoculars, bug protection, plastic bag to pick up litter, tree, flower and bird guides

Scenic Delights:
The Greenbelt Is this really possible in New York City? You can walk almost entirely through forest along a 35-mile trail network that is crossed only by several minor roads. Here is a wild natural area containing about 18 ponds, 24 distinct knolls and hills (including the highest hill on the U.S. Atlantic seaboard -- see p. 42), a dozen surprisingly clean brooks and five concentrations of ancient trees. The 3,000-acre Greenbelt City Park is one of the largest city parks of any eastern U.S. city, larger than Central, Prospect and Van Cortlandt Parks combined.

The central portion of the Greenbelt, part of which is described here, runs from Rockland Avenue to the border with St. Francis Woodlands.

Tour of the Glacial Ponds Each of the six six ponds and wetlands visited by this tour is distinct from the others. Loosestrife Swamp is covered by--you guessed it--swamp loosestrife. The 16-acre Ohrbach Lake is deep and mostly open water, except for several bays covered by aquatic plants. Tiny, insect-eating bladderwort fills Pumphouse Pond. Hourglass Pond has an hour-glass shape and is covered by white water lily and ferny cabomba. Duckweed Pond is covered in summer by a delicate green coating of duckweed, the world's smallest wildflower. Frog Pond is partly covered by duckweed and arrow arum.

The Greenbelt's glacial ponds were created 15,000 years ago when the Ice Age glacier melted away, leaving colossal blocks of ice

Central Greenbelt

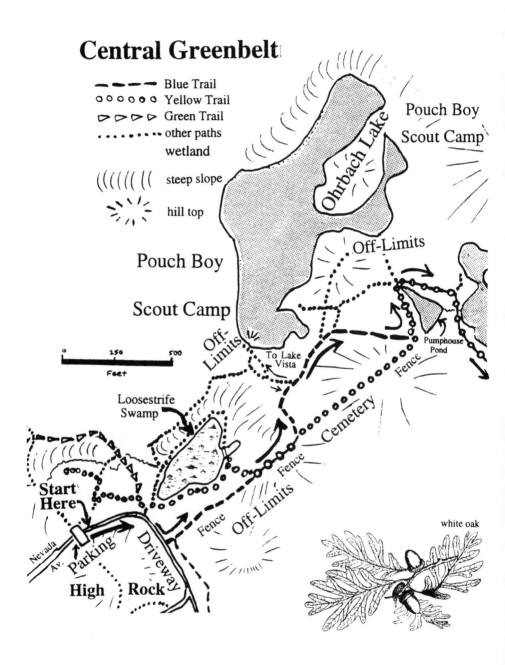

- **– – – –** Blue Trail
- **ooooooo** Yellow Trail
- **▷▷▷▷** Green Trail
- **••••••••** other paths
- wetland
- **((((((((** steep slope
- hill top

Ohrbach Lake

Pouch Boy
Scout Camp

Pouch Boy

Scout Camp

Off-Limits

Off-Limits

To Lake Vista

Pumphouse Pond

Loosestrife Swamp

Cemetery

Fence

Fence

Off-Limits

Start Here

Nevada Av.

Parking

Driveway

High Rock

Fence

white oak

Feet

0   250   500

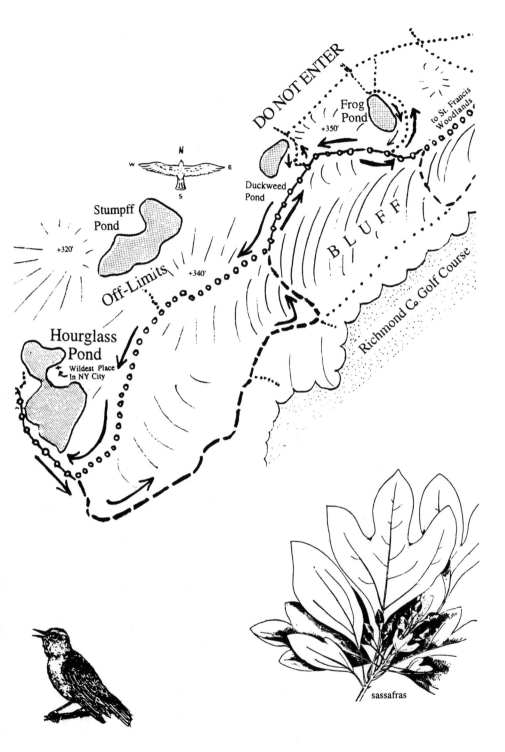

DO NOT ENTER

Frog
Pond
+350'

to St. Francis
Woodlands

Duckweed
Pond

N
W   E
S

Stumpff
Pond

+320'

Off-Limits
+340'

B L U F F

Richmond Co. Golf Course

Hourglass
Pond

Wildest Place
In NY City

sassafras

scattered across certain areas. These blocks occupied depressions surrounded by higher piles and layers of gravel and rock debris (moraine) that settled into knolls and ridges. When the giant "ice cubes" melted away, their depressions (called kettle holes) often remained filled with water.

The Wildest Place in NY City   The wildest natural point in the five boroughs is located in the central Greenbelt. "Wildest" refers here to that natural point on land (not water or marsh) that is the most remote from streets or homes. The wildest place, to be precise, is near the Yellow Trail just north of Hourglass Pond.

Stately Old Trees   The portion of the central Greenbelt between St. Francis and High Rock contains several areas of impressive trees that date back to at least the mid-1800s. Three-to four-foot diameter tulip trees, red and white oak and beech are concentrated along the trail to the north of Hourglass and east of Stumpff Ponds.

Haven For Wildlife   Wildlife finds large areas of natural habitat and freedom from human disturbance in this remote refuge. In spring and fall, it's a treasure trove for warblers and other migrating birds. Herons, egrets, wood ducks and large turtles frequent the isolated ponds. Rare royal and fragile fern, bloodroot and whorled pogonia are a few of the unusual plants here.

How to Get There:

By Bus: From the Ferry, take the S74 bus to Rose Avenue to transfer to S57 bus to Rockland Avenue. The S54 also goes to Nevada Avenue. Walk a half-mile to the end of Nevada Avenue.

By Car: Take Richmond Road to Rockland Avenue. On Rockland, drive 0.4 mile to Nevada Avenue. (Watch carefully for it!) Turn right on Nevada and drive to the end.

Park in the High Rock parking lot. Walk through the gates and up the park driveway. Where it starts to bend sharply right, notice the little clearing on the left side with a pile of wood chips. Several foot paths meet here. Walk 30 feet to the opposite end of the clearing and take the left fork (*an unblazed path -- if the trail is blazed, you are on the wrong one*). You quickly will see the swamp on your right. At the opposite end of **Loosestrife Swamp**, an open boardwalk will provide you with a full view: a glacial kettle pond completely covered with tall loosestrife.

Immediately after the boardwalk, *watch for the first left-hand path*. In 50 feet, it meets the Blue Blaze Trail and a high fence. Turn *left* and follow along the fence. On the other side of the fence are magnificent white pine and oaks on the grounds of the Vanderbilt

Cemetery. Shortly after it starts up a hill, the trail bends to the left (don't continue along the fence).

It climbs through shady oak forest and then levels out. It is soon joined by a trail from the left -- the Red Dot Trail (red dot inside white rectangle). Take a temporary excursion off the Blue Trail by turning left on the Red Dot Trail. In 300 feet, you enter a grassy clearing in 200 feet. Walk to its opposite side and then look to the right for a wide path. In 100 feet, you arrive at the shore of 16-acre **sparkling Ohrbach Lake**. (Although you will see a "Boy Scout Property - No Trespassing" sign, you are on public land up to the south shore of the lake. **Don't go any further!** The Scouts own all the rest of the lake and the sign is intended to keep intruders from exploring further.)

Across the lake are the Berlin Scout Lodge, dock and beach, serving thousands of scouts annually -- their wilderness in the city. The 90-acre camp is the last large private inholding in the Greenbelt. The Scouts are aware of the natural treasure they hold and it is hoped they will not ever convey the land to developers in the future. Show your respect and quietly return the way you came.

When you're back to the Blue Trail, turn left. You will pass by tall shrubs of highbush blueberry -- great to eat in midsummer! The large oaks towering over you have very little vegetation below them. It has been kept relatively barren by past camping and motorcycles years ago. Stay on the Blue Trail when the Red Dot Trail forks left.

The Blue Trail will arrive at **Pumphouse Pond**. Note that the Yellow Trail comes in from the right and joins the Blue Trail (see the blazes on a large boulder). Bear left on the trail which now has both blue and yellow blazes. Observe the concrete foundation of the building on the lake edge which once pumped water to High Rock.

The Blue and Yellow Trail rounds the edge of the pond and then meets the fence of Moravian Cemetery. Moments later, you are at **Hourglass Pond**. It was named because it is two separate ponds connected by a skinny waterway. The shape is only visible in fall or winter; to see it, you must walk the edge of the pond (no path). Approach quietly; this is a haven for herons , ducks and turtles.

Devil's Walking Stick

Shortly after you leave the lake, the Yellow Trail separates to the left. Stay on the Blue Trail. Note the large oaks, the twitter of birds -- and the devil's walking stick. This is the shrub with tall stems coated with long thorns. After the Blue Trail descends Todt Hill's bluff, you parallel the Richmond County Golf Course, visible through the trees to your right. Enjoy the **large stately trees** on either side.

This bottom-of-the-hill trail is buggier than the dry upland woods. Make sure you turn onto the next left-hand trail (still blue blazed). It will climb back up the hill, passing square piles of rock, remnants of a former country home. At a flat clearing with a tree in the middle, the Yellow Trail meets it again. Turn right on the Blue (and Yellow) Trail.

It heads up another rise again. When you reach the top, look for a small path on your left that heads steeply downhill to a pond which you can see below. Turn down this foot path to visit your fifth pond, **Duckweed Pond**. (Quiet ....wood ducks could be there!) Enjoy the seclusion and serenity here. Return up the hill to the Blue Trail again and turn left.

Walk exactly 130 steps to the next left-hand path. Again, quietly follow it down to see **Frog Pond**. As a child at Camp Kaufman, the author caught gobs of frogs here every summer. Do not follow any other paths because they all enter Camp property.

Return to the Blue and Yellow Trail and turn *right*. (If you head left and follow the Blue Trail, you will reach the **overlook vista** (see p. 50). Turn right at the gravel road and walk to its end).

On your way back, follow the Yellow blazes. When you return to the little clearing with the single tree in the middle, the Blue Trail cuts off to the left. You take the Yellow Trail straight ahead (not well blazed at time of visit). The Yellow Trail traverses the high ridge, passing other out-of-sight ponds to your right. You are now at the **wildest (dry) spot in all of NY City**: 1,700 feet from the nearest public street or home to the east or west, 3,200 feet to the north, and 2,500 feet to the south.

Soon, the Yellow Trail rejoins the Blue Trail. Turn right, following yellow and blue blazes. You pass by Hourglass Pond again. As the trail curves left around Pumphouse Pond, ignore the paths to the right, which lead into Scout property.

At the opposite end of Pumphouse Pond, be sure to watch for where the Blue Trail cuts off to the right (while the Yellow Trail continues ahead to meet the cemetery fence).

Follow the Blue Trail back all the way. After reaching the cemetery fence, you reach the High Rock driveway. Turn right and you quickly arrive at the parking lot.

For information, or to help protect the Greenbelt, contact:
- Protectors of Pine Oak Woods
- Urban Trail Club   see addresses in appendix
- Greenbelt Park

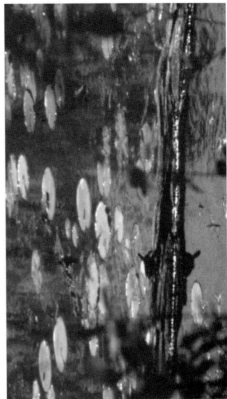

Turtles and water lilies on Walker
Pond, High Rock Park

Ohrbach Lake, a wild jewel in the
heart of the Greenbelt

HIGH ROCK, GEM OF THE GREENBELT

Ramble over knobby glacial hills through the "Gem of the Greenbelt," past peaceful ponds and wildlife-rich wetlands. See the place where the Greenbelt Park -- and Staten Island's save-the-parks movement -- was born. Enjoy the programs of the environmental center that has been nationally recognized as a "National Environmental Education Landmark."

Distance: 1.7 miles for the Pond Loop; 0.7 miles for the Brook Loop

Level of Difficulty: easy to moderate. The Pond Loop has a return climb of 160 feet; the West Loop climbs up and down 25-foot slopes.

Things to Bring: a sense of beauty, camera, binoculars, bird, tree and flower guides, bug protection, plastic bag for litter pick-up. Know your poison ivy (occasional here).

Scenic Delights:
   The Place Where the Greenbelt Was Born High Rock Park is where the vast natural area, later to become the Staten Island Greenbelt Park, was born. The attempted destruction of High Rock is also the historical event that triggered Staten Island's environmental movement and public support for park protection -- six years *before* the first National Earth Day in 1970.
   Most of the presently protected nearly 3000 acres of Greenbelt, Bluebelt and other park land owe their existence to this local environmental movement. Represented today by Protectors of Pine Oak Woods and allied other groups, the grassroots effort has struggled and campaigned for 34 years against the greatest of odds: well-financed developers, short-sighted public officials, a seemingly omnipotent highway lobby -- and the relentless pressure of urban sprawl from the country's largest city.
   The Verrazano Bridge and Staten Island Expressway had just opened in 1964-1965 when a developer announced plans to build high-rise apartments on the just-sold former High Rock Girl Scout Camp. Rather than helplessly watch the scenic heart of the Greenbelt be destroyed, a committed group of citizens, led by Greta Moulton, waged a campaign to purchase High Rock. They procured more than $1.2 million and High Rock appeared to have been saved.
   But this first success wasn't sufficient. Planned construction of expressways would destroy the entire Greenbelt, including High Rock, Latourette and Willowbrook Parks, and Richmond Town.

Four months after High Rock was purchased, Governor Nelson Rockefeller visited High Rock. He was confronted with the question, "Governor, what are you going to do about a state highway planned to cut through these woods between High Rock and Pouch Boy Scout Camp?"

Thus began the intense struggle to stop the planned expressways and save the Greenbelt. As success built upon success, Staten Island park and nature lovers expanded their campaign to protect *southern* Staten Island's scenic gems. In 1973, Protectors of Pine Oak Woods was formed initially to save Clay Pit Ponds (now the Island's only state park). After court battles, public campaigns, and struggle after struggle, Greenbelt Park was created in 1984. After that, citizens also saved an entire complex of "Bluebelt" parks in the south, and wildlife reserves in the north.

That first success started here at High Rock. Because of caring, committed citizens, Staten Island's and New York City's residents have been enriched forevermore.

Scenic Gem With Five Ponds and Wetlands High Rock possesses a classical natural beauty found in few cities. This is definitely one place that has not changed, a refuge oblivious to bridge tolls and traffic jams. Stately old trees line the trails which meander past five scenic ponds and wetlands. Crystal clear streams (in New York City !!) gurgle to the cheerful calls of abundant bird life, toads, frogs, cicadas and other members of Nature's chorus.

National Environmental Education Landmark As a superlative center for the nature and ecology instruction, High Rock was recognized by the U.S. government in 1971 as a National Environmental Education Landmark. It offers programs and tours for park visitors, including 10,000 children a year. A unique Fragrant Garden for the Visually Handicapped is one of three gardens near the Visitor Center. A soil research lab and headquarters for the Urban Park Rangers (currently reduced because of budget cuts) are other facilities.

Rich Wildlife and Wildflowers The five ponds are magnets for wildlife, including the elusive wood duck and great blue heron, as well as hawks, owls, muskrat, migrating colorful warblers, woodpeckers, frogs, turtles and more. Fragrant pinxter azalea, sweet pepperbush, highbush blueberry, the bizarre skunk cabbage and a myriad of other wildflowers await you.

skunk cabbage

How to Get There:

By Bus: From the Ferry, take S74 bus to Rose Avenue; then transfer to S57 bus to Rockland Avenue. Walk a third of a mile to the end of Nevada Avenue.

Pouch Boy Scout Camp

Off-Limits

Off-Limits

to Mt. Moses

To Mt. Moses

Manor Rd.

Persimmon Grove

Giant Glacial Boulder

Loosestrife Swamp

to Central Greenwich

2

Start Here
(Parking)

Nevada Av.

1

+260'

Fence

Cemetery

Fence

High Rock Park

250   500

Feet

High Rock Park

① **Pond Loop Walk**
② **Brook Loop Walk**

– – – – **Blue Trail**
oooooo **Yellow Trail**
▷▷▷▷▷ **Green Trail**
●●●●●● **Red Trail**
>>>>>> **White Trail**
······· **unmarked paths**
= = = = **woods road**
//////(**steep slope**
⸝⸜⸝⸜ **hill top**
~~~ **wetland**

Vis. Ctr.

Park HQ

Fence

Tonking

to Egbertville Ravine

Walker Pond

Altamont Pond

Light House

Altamont

Boyle

Turtle Pond

Beacon

Summit Av.

W N S E

By Car: Take Richmond Road to Rockland Avenue. On Rockland, drive 0.4 mile to Nevada Avenue. Turn right on Nevada and drive to the end.

Two trail loops are suggested, one to High Rock's five ponds, the other along babbling brooks. You can combine them into a larger loop if desired.

The Tour of Ponds:
From the Nevada Avenue parking lot, walk through the gates and up the driveway. At the place where the road sharply veers right, proceed straight (where there might be a big wood chip pile). At the fork, take the unblazed path which follows the left side of **Loosestrife Swamp.** About 200 feet after you started on

Boardwalk, Loosestrife Swamp, High Rock

the path, look for a left-hand path that leads to a huge boulder 75 feet away. This boulder was shoved here by the Ice Age glaciers 15,000 years ago! Walk up to it to inspect it, but return to the path.

The path winds around the swamp and reaches a foot bridge across one end. Walk silently so you won't scare off wildlife! Be ready with binoculars. Note the swamp loosestrife that covers the pond. Only 15 to 20 years ago, the pond was much more open water.

Pinch yourself (not too hard!) as a reminder that you are still in NY City! This is one of the city's wildest locations! As you follow the path around the swamp, the Yellow Trail joins it from the left. Continue until it returns to the place you started. Walk onto the park drive and turn left. Only 50 feet further, the Blue Trail is visible ten steps to your left. Go to the blue blaze (framed in white) and take it to the right. Note the fence that separates High Rock from the private Vanderbilt Cemetery.

In a few minutes, the Blue Trail veers right and joins the driveway. **However, you continue straight on the unblazed path**. It becomes white-blazed and leads you downhill along the cemetery fence and past majestic tulip trees, then past a little vernal

swamp loosestrife

(springtime) pool along a boardwalk. Follow the white-blazed path down pretty, rolling glacial hills, ignoring side paths.

At the bottom of the hill, you reach an old fire road. Turn right and you pass a house (stay away -- private!). Watch for **Altamont Pond** through the woods on your left. The first path on your left circles around to the pond's other end, where if you are quiet, you may surprise some birds or turtles. If you go far enough, you will see an opening through a fence. Boyle Street is on the other side. Walk out of the woods onto the road. Look up to your left and you will see something unexpected -- a yellow **lighthouse**! It is privately owned but is enjoyable to look at.

Return to the fire road. Make the next left onto another side path. Take it to see **Turtle Pond**. After wildlife watching, return again to the fire road and turn left on it. (Note: the fire road changes to a blue blaze and also a "red paw" blaze.) **Walker Pond** now comes into view. The next left side path goes to it. Take time to meditate on the dock and watch animals on the pond. It is known for lots of turtles, lily pads, mallard, and if you're lucky, wood duck, heron, glossy ibis and black-crowned night heron. Enjoy the rustle of the leaves and the serenity. You can circle the pond. One path on the right leads to a little-used parking lot off Summit Avenue.

Go back to the fire road. (If you turn left, the Blue Trail reaches the dead-end of Tonking Road, leads to Rockland Avenue and continues to points south.) You turn right and follow the Red Paw Trail to get back to where you began.

Follow the fire road to where the Red Paw Trail turns left. It climbs steeply through towering trees and ends up at the Roosevelt Lab and **Environmental Education Center**. When you step onto the driveway, note the woman's restroom building opposite the Environmental Center. Proceed only up to the further corner of the restroom building, then turn left on the unblazed path that goes behind the restroom.

The path climbs through dry oak woods to the top of a hill, then descends sharply. You are now at the parking lot.

The Brook Loop:
Locate this trailhead from the Nevada Avenue parking lot as follows: when you are facing the exit, look to your right at the nearest corner of the parking lot. That is where a wide unmarked path begins. Take it down to wooden benches in the woods. Head downhill to Moulton Brook, but don't cross it. This is where you connect with the Yellow Trail. Turn left.

The Yellow Trail soon makes a very sharp right turn and then crosses a wooden walk over a swampy area. This tall forest of sweet gum, black oak, black birch and thorny brier is one of the finest in NY City. The Yellow Trail then crosses a wooden bridge over the brook. The source of this pristine brook is Loosestrife Swamp -- in other words, it has no source of human pollution!

From the wooden bridge, count *exactly 100 steps.* At this point, you will see another brook on your left. You are now standing under a rare grove of **persimmons**, a southern tree at its northern limits here. You can identify it by its bark, which has neat rows of little knobs. Persimmon fruit is edible when it ripens around Thanksgiving.

Continue on the Yellow Trail and you pass through a scrubby field filled with dense brier. Then you re-enter a mature forest and arrive at a fork (why not a knife?). (If you turn left, you'll cross a bridge and reach Manor Road. Across Manor is the trail that takes you up Mt. Moses, described on p. 72.)

Turn right on the Green Trail. Pass through a red maple and oak forest. After crossing a little brook, bear right, following the Green Trail. From now on, ignore unmarked paths and always watch for green blazes. On the top of a ridge, the Green Trail splits and the two parts rejoin each other in 200 feet.

When you reach a grassy opening at the top of the moraine ridge, notice the glacially transported boulders are made of granite and red shale (not native to Staten Island). Bear right, following the Green Trail down a 50-foot slope. At a trail junction marked by an oak with three separate trunks, bear right and follow the Green Trail straight ahead to a little foot bridge. You arrive at a clearing with benches and wood chip pile.

Turn left onto the path that follows the margin of the swamp, which is on your right. At the opposite end of Loosestrife Swamp is a wooden foot bridge, perfect for viewing wildlife. Continue circling the swamp until you return to the beginning of the swamp path loop. Now proceed to the park driveway ahead (**watch out for cars!**).

If you want to return to your car, walk downhill to the parking lot. If you want to continue on the Pond Loop, turn left on the park driveway, walk 50 yards and turn left onto the Blue Trail. Follow the directions for the Pond Loop route from here on.

For information, and to help protect the Greenbelt, contact:
- Protectors of Pine Oak Woods   see addresses
- Greenbelt Park (for programs)   in
- Urban Trail Club (to assist in blazing trails)   appendix
- Greenbelt Conservancy

MT. MOSES AND THE MILLION DOLLAR VIEW

Marvel at Mt. Moses' awe-inspiring panorama, a 360-degree view of the best Staten Island has to offer. Admire the entire Greenbelt at your feet! Spiral up Mt. Moses, once part of a massive highway project, now a monument to the defeat of the highway that would have destroyed the Greenbelt. Wonder at the mysterious rock inscriptions, and try to decipher them. Thrill to the sight of dozens of hawks soaring by during migration season.

Distance: 1.25 miles round trip

Level of Difficulty: easy for the first half, then a moderate 110-foot climb

Things to Bring: a love of panoramas; binoculars, camera, bird guide, bug protection, plastic bags to pick up litter. Know your poison ivy (occasional here).

Scenic Delights:
Mt. Moses Created in controversy, Mt. Moses is now one of New York City's premier scenic view points. It is unique in several ways. It's Staten Island's only natural 360-degree panorama. In every direction is a virtually natural landscape, evoking another one of those "I can't believe I'm in New York City!" comments. Last is the irony .... it was created to build a highway that would have destroyed the Greenbelt. Now it is one of the Greenbelt's most outstanding assets.

In 1963, during construction of the S.I. Expressway, huge amounts of rock were blasted away. Much of this rock, more than *50,000 tons* of it, was piled up at the foot of Manor Road. The intention was to use it to fill in Greenbelt valleys so the highway could cross them. While lovers of the Greenbelt battled the highway lobby for 20 years, the steep hill of serpentine boulders became a favorite destination of hikers. By the time the highway was defeated, the hill had become covered with a stunted forest, except for its bare summit. It was named Mt. Moses as a tongue-in-cheek jab at Robert F. Moses, the primary supporter of the highway project (see p.44 for details).

The 360-Degree Panorama From atop Mt. Moses, a pristine carpet of green stretches out like a carpet in all directions. Five hills undulate on the horizon: Lighthouse Hill to the south, Heyerdahl Hill to the west, Seaview Hill to the north, High Rock to the east and Todt Hill to the northeast. Only two man-made structures can clearly

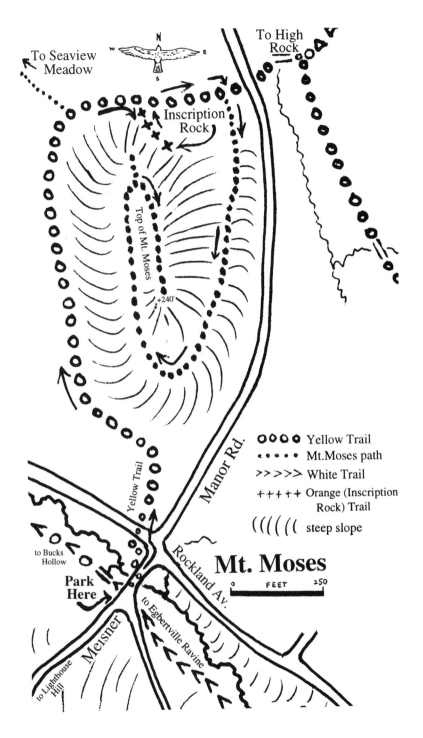

To Seaview
Meadow

N
W E
S

To High
Rock

Inscription
Rock

Top of Mt. Moses

+240'

Manor Rd.

Yellow Trail

to Bucks
Hollow

**Park
Here**

Rockland Av.

Meisner

to Egbertville Ravine

to Lighthouse Hill

O O O O Yellow Trail
• • • • • Mt.Moses path
> > > > > White Trail
+ + + + + Orange (Inscription
Rock) Trail
((((((steep slope

Mt. Moses

0 FEET 250

Mt. Moses Vista

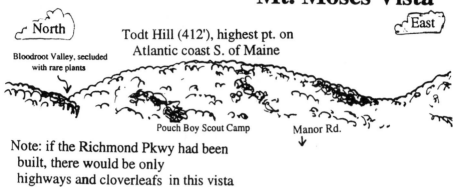

North

Bloodroot Valley, secluded
with rare plants

Todt Hill (412'), highest pt. on
Atlantic coast S. of Maine

East

Pouch Boy Scout Camp

Manor Rd.

Note: if the Richmond Pkwy had been
built, there would be only
highways and cloverleafs in this vista

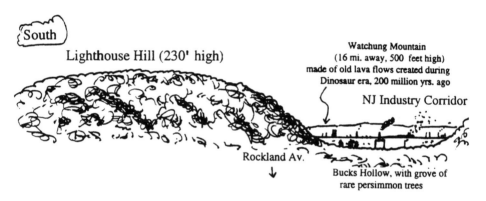

South

Lighthouse Hill (230' high)

Watchung Mountain
(16 mi. away, 500 feet high)
made of old lava flows created during
Dinosaur era, 200 million yrs. ago

NJ Industry Corridor

Rockland Av.

Bucks Hollow, with grove of
rare persimmon trees

be seen -- Seaview Hospital and the Eger Lutheran Nursing Home. To the southeast, on a clear day, New Jersey's Atlantic Highlands and Sandy Hook can be seen 15 miles away. To the west, you can barely see New Jersey's industry row, five miles away.

The Mysterious Rock Inscriptions When the author explored Mt. Moses as a youth, he stumbled upon mysterious inscriptions on a boulder, written in an unknown alphabet. They lay hidden on a boulder-filled slope for 30 years, unbeknownst to virtually anybody else. In the writing of this book, the author spent a long time trying to find them again. Now you can view them for yourself. See if you can translate them and reveal their wise saying!

The Hawk-Watching Spectacle Mt. Moses is the place to be to watch hawks (such as red-tail and Cooper's), threatened osprey and other birds of prey during the September and spring migrations. They flap and soar by, sometimes dozen in an hour. If you are lucky,

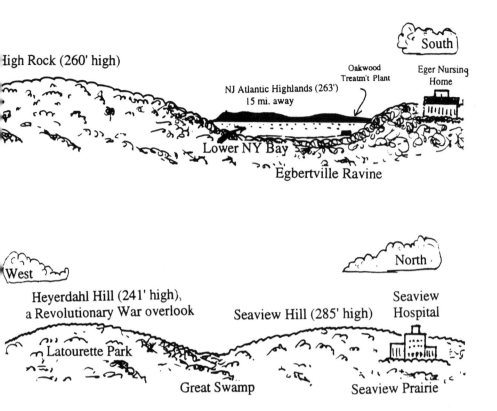

High Rock (260' high)

South

Oakwood
Treatm't Plant

Eger Nursing
Home

NJ Atlantic Highlands (263')
15 mi. away

Lower NY Bay

Egbertville Ravine

West

North

Heyerdahl Hill (241' high),
a Revolutionary War overlook

Seaview Hill (285' high)

Seaview
Hospital

Latourette Park

Great Swamp

Seaview Prairie

you may even see a rare eagle.

If you are not experienced in watching birds, the ideal way to do it is with a "guided" tour. Contact the S.I. Institute, NY City Audubon or Protectors (listed in appendix) to learn about their scheduled birding trips. Just join the field trip; their experts know exactly when to go and they will identify the birds for you.

How to Get There:

By Bus: Take the S54 or 57 to the intersection of Rockland Avenue and Manor Road. To orient which way to the trail, do this: if you stand looking *toward* Manor Road, head to your left along Rockland. In 100 feet, turn into the clearing with a metal barricade.

By Car: From the east, take the S.I. Expressway to Todt Hill Road Exit. Drive straight along Service Road to Manor Road. Turn left on Manor. From the west, take Bradley Avenue exit. Drive straight along service road until it ends at Manor Road. Make a right on Manor. Drive on Manor until it ends at Rockland Avenue. Cross Rockland onto Meisner Avenue and park immediately.

If you parked on Meisner, walk down Meisner to Rockland Avenue. Cross it at the light, then turn left on Rockland. Walk 100 feet to a clearing on the right where there is a metal barrier into the woods. **Rockland is very dangerous -- take extreme caution and walk clear off the road to avoid cars!**

Walk around the steel barrier onto the Yellow Trail. At the little Seaview Hospital Gas House, make a left. The Yellow Trail will enter a forest of sweet gum and red maple. **Steer clear of poison ivy.** Watch for the devil's walking stick, a tall shrub you can't miss -- its tall straight stem could make a perfect walking staff except for one thing: it's armored with thousands of stout needles. Hence the name!

As you walk, notice the **giant green boulders of serpentine** to the right. You are circling around the bottom of Mt. Moses which rises 110 feet above you.

Devils
Walkin

When your reach a path on your left, bear right (are there really bears on the right?!), staying on the Yellow Trail. In 200 feet, watch for the orange-blazed side trail on your right. The Orange Trail leads you in 300 feet to the **mysterious rock inscriptions**. For the last 100 feet, you will have to climb over boulders past pyramid rock piles that date back to the time of the inscriptions. **Don't deface the inscriptions so others can enjoy them.**

Return to the Yellow Trail and turn right. Watch for the next path to your right (if you reach the road, you've gone too far). This is the unblazed Mt. Moses Path. It spirals around the hill up to the summit. When you are on the top ridge, watch for a path on the left (just before it turns sharply right). In 100 feet this dead-end path arrives at a pile of giant, jagged boulders and a **clear view** northward. **Watch out for poison ivy.**

Sumac

After this side trip, the path quickly takes you along the summit ridge. Notice the scrubby trees of sumac, tree of heaven, and cherry. They grow poorly because there is almost no soil here, mostly boulders, and the boulders are mostly serpentine -- noted for being very infertile and even toxic due to high amounts of nickel.

When you reach the pinnacle, admire the **stunning 360-degree panorama**. Pinch yourself (not *too* hard!) to remind yourself that you're on a green island in an ocean of 17 million people! You are seeing the Greenbelt spread out before your eyes. Imagine what this would have looked like if Robert Moses had gotten his way: a network of highways and cloverleafs, the roar of traffic, sprawling shoulder-to-shoulder subdivisions and strip malls. Most of the park land would have been gone ... forever.

If you come on a clear day, see if Sandy Hook is visible. Use your binoculars for the vista as well as for birdwatching,

View of NJ Highlands, 15 miles away, from Mt. Moses

especially the **hawk spectacle** in spring and fall.

When you're done drinking in the view, return the way you came. The Mt. Moses path will reach the Yellow Trail. (If you turn right on the Yellow Trail and cross Manor Road, the trail takes you into High Rock.) You turn left on the Yellow Trail and follow it back to Rockland Avenue. **Remember the hazardous traffic!**

For information, or to help protect the Greenbelt, contact:
- Protectors of Pine Oak Woods
- Sierra Club   see addresses
- Greenbelt Park   in appendix
- Urban Trail Club (to assist trail blazing)
- Audubon Society (for hawk watching trips)

View of the Catskills? No!... the view from Staten Island's Mt. Moses

EGBERTVILLE RAVINE AND LIGHTHOUSE HILL: EXQUISITE WILDNESS, EXQUISITE HOMES

Delight in a charming forest and babbling brook. Appreciate the exquisite homes and gardens of Lighthouse Hill. Treat yourself to the sight of the Lighthouse and Frank Lloyd Wright home. Relish the exotic splendor of the world-class art of the Tibetan Museum. Walk the upper part of the Amundsen Trailway, which could become the Greenbelt's route to the sea in the future.

Distance: 2.5 miles round trip

Level of Difficulty: relatively easy except the 10-minute climb up Meisner Avenue.

Things to Bring: an appreciation of the elegant and artistic; camera, binoculars, plastic bags to pick up litter, bird and flower guides, bug protection. Know your poison ivy (occasional).

Scenic Delights:
Egbertville Ravine Reminiscent of a tumbling Catskill mountain brook, Egbertville Ravine is another place where you wonder "Can this really be New York City?" Richmond Creek, which begins in Camp Kaufman, continues to carve and deepen this narrow ravine that was originally cut by the massive meltwaters pouring off the Ice Age glacier 15,000 years ago. What adds to Egbertville Ravine's beauty are the ancient tulip trees, beech and red oak that line it. This makes it one of the three oldest forests in Staten Island. The age of one four-foot diameter tulip tree was measured at exactly 200 years old (!). Others could also date back to 1800 or earlier. What makes this surprising is that around 1900, the stream was dammed and a small pond filled part of the ravine. That pond was built to power a sawmill. Yet neither the flooding nor the sawmill led to cutting of the old-growth trees.

Amundsen Trailway The Amundsen Trailway project was conceived in 1974 when the S.I. Greenbelt Natural Areas League (predecessor of Protectors of Pine Oak Woods) held a public walk for officials and the media. At the time, the 4.5-mile undeveloped corridor was still projected to become the Willowbrook Expressway; this and the Richmond Parkway would have destroyed the Greenbelt if built. Park supporters pushed for it to become a trailway to link walkers and bicyclists from the Greenbelt to Great Kills Park, from the forest to the sea.

City officials have still not dropped the idea of some kind of through road, even though the corridor is part of a city plan for a

Egbertville Ravine & Light House Hill

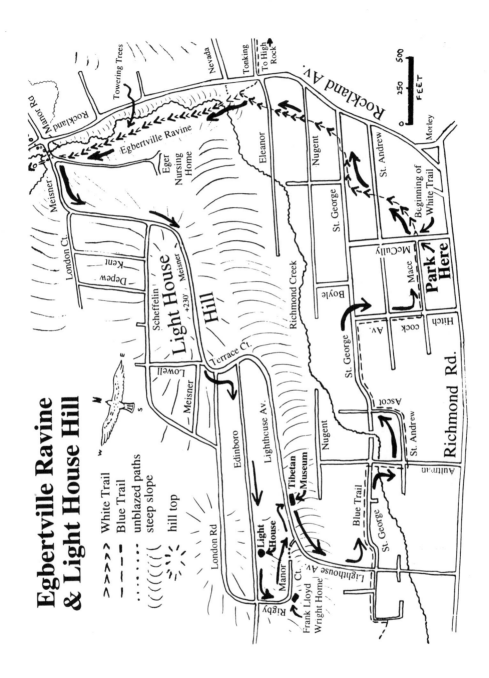

- >>>> White Trail
- – – – Blue Trail
- ·········· unblazed paths
-)))) steep slope
- hill top

Light House Hill +230'

Egbertville Ravine

Eger Nursing Home

Richmond Creek

Tibetan Museum

Light House

Frank Lloyd Wright Home

Park Here

Beginning of White Trail

To High Rock

Rockland Av.

Richmond Rd.

0   250   500 FEET

borough-wide bike and walking path and the city Parks Department now administers it. After 34 years, the destructive "parkway" project has not died, but the trailway project has not quite been born.

However, hikers and local residents use the White Trail, (built and maintained by the Urban Trail Club) that traverses the north half of the right-of-way corridor.

Although he is not historically associated with the trailway, it was named after Roald Amundsen to honor the Norwegian discoverer of the South Pole. You can see a monument to him on the trail corridor at the intersection of Amboy Road and Clarke Avenue.

The Lighthouse and Lighthouse Hill Rising 220 feet above Richmond Road, Lighthouse Hill is one of the Greenbelt's dozen major hills. The hill is named after the Lighthouse (built in 1912 and still in operation) whose beacon can be seen far out to sea. Enjoy the light house from the road. Although the U.S. Coast Guard owns the lighthouse, the lighthouse keeper's house is private. Lighthouse Hill is also noted for its neighborhood of elegant homes and landscaping.

The Tibetan Museum and the Frank Lloyd Wright House Lighthouse Hill is famous for more than its lighthouse. The Jacques Marchais Museum of Tibetan Art, at 338 Lighthouse Avenue, houses the largest collection of Tibetan art outside Tibet. Its stunning buildings and landscaping are matched by the exotic beauty of its Tibetan statues, paintings and ceremonial objects. You can visit the must-see, globally unique museum as part of this walk.

It is open Wed.-Sun. 1- 5 pm (April through November); from December through March, open by appointment (718-987-3500) Wed. - Fri., 1 - 5 pm. There is a nominal fee.

The Frank Lloyd Wright House (called Crimson Beech) is New York City's only private home built by the world's most famous 20th century architect. You can appreciate the unique style and beauty of the private home from the road.

How to Get There:

By Rapid Transit: Exit at Oakwood Heights Station. Head north on Guyon Avenue to Amboy Road. Make a left on Amboy, go one block, make a right on Reidel Avenue. At Bishop Street (the only street on your left), turn left and cross Richmond Road to McCully Street; walk one block to Mace Street.

By Bus: Take the S54 or 74 to McCully Street (off Richmond Road). Walk one block to Mace Street.

By Car: From the Verrazano Bridge, take the S.I. Expressway to Richmond Road Exit. Take the Service Road to Richmond Road. Turn left on Richmond Rd.

From the west along the S.I. Expressway, get off at Clove Road-Richmond Road Exit. Take the Service Road to Richmond Road and make a right.

Following Richmond Road, pass the intersection with Rockland Avenue.

Credit: Jack Baird

Can this be New York City? Winter serenity along babbling brook, Egbertville Ravine

In one block, turn right on McCully Street. Park at McCully and Mace St.

The Blue Trail comes in from Mace Street and joins the White Trail at the intersection with McCully Street. Look for the blue rectangle trail blaze on the telephone pole on McCully Street *directly opposite where* Mace Street meets it. This is where the White Trail begins. Together, the Blue and White Trail enters a forest of red maple, sassafras, cherry, and black and swamp white oaks. Look for the edible wild garlic. When the trail crosses St. Andrews Road, look across the street for the blue and white blaze and continue. Observe a vine-covered cellar hole to the left, the remains of a former home.

When you near the next street (St. George), do not cross. The trail turns right and parallels St. George for 200 yards. When you reach the street, turn right and follow the road 50 feet Then cross to the other side of the road where you see brick steps (the remnants of another home demolished in the 1950s for the would-be expressway). Cross Nugent and follow the trail up hill. (At Eleanor Street, the Blue Trail separates from the White Trail and heads to the right across Rockland Avenue and enters High Rock Park at Tonking Road.) At the fire hydrant, the White Trail enters the stately forest at the edge of the Greenbelt.

Moments later, you are overlooking a great red oak (with a tattered rope hanging from it) and the bubbling brook of Richmond Creek and Egbertville Ravine. The ravine was named after Cornelius Egbert, a member of Staten Island's 1820s infantry unit.

Cross the wooden footbridge and marvel at the size of the **200-year-old tulip trees** as you travel along the stream and up **Egbertville Ravine**. Walk off the trail to touch one and feel its primeval massiveness and deeply furrowed bark. Try to sense the ancientness of the place.

tulip tree

When the White Trail leaves the forest 1,400 feet later, walk 50 feet ahead to Meisner Avenue and turn left. You are now touring the Lighthouse Hill neighborhood. **The road is curving and narrow -- take caution and stay clear of cars. Respect the privacy of the residents; walk quietly and stay on the road.**

Climb 80 feet higher as Meisner Avenue ascends the hill past beautiful homes. The road will curve left (now called Terrace Court). In one block, turn right on Edinboro Road. Admire the attractive mansions and gardens. Walk 0.4 mile to 402 Edinboro Road to see **the Lighthouse** that the hill is named after. Its beacon still shines toward the Lower Bay.

The Lighthouse

Continue on Edinboro till it reaches Rigby Street. Turn left. (The best photo of the Lighthouse is from Manor Ct.) Follow Rigby and make the next left onto Manor Court. From the curb, stop to see the first house on your right (48 Manor Court) (private -- do not enter). This is **Crimson Beech, the only private home in New York City built by Frank Lloyd Wright**, the world-famous architect. Notice its long, low-slung layout with redwood frames, a typical Wright architecture.

Walk to the end of Manor Court. As you walk past the metal barricade at its end, notice the rather large white oak. Follow the path until it joins a cobble road. You are now at the lower slope below the Lighthouse. When you reach Lighthouse Avenue, turn left. Walk on Lighthouse Avenue, counting three houses on your right. The entrance of the Jacques Marchais **Museum of Tibetan Art** is on your right, immediately after 340 Lighthouse Avenue.

When it is open, a large sign will identify it. You must enter through a metal gate to the right of a long low wall. If it is not open, it cannot be seen from the road. Be sure to see this unique, off-beat small museum! Its hours are listed previously.

From the Tibetan Museum, *go back down Lighthouse Avenue the way you came.* As you walk down the very steep, curving road, keep to your left and watch for cars (**CAUTION!**) At the bottom of the hill, it turns to the left.

At the first intersection, turn left on St. George Road. You have rejoined the Blue Trail. Watch for blazes on telephone poles. At the next four-way intersection, turn right on Aultman (follow the blue blazes). Cross Richmond Creek, then turn left on St. Andrew Road.

On your left for several blocks, notice Richmond Creek and its Bluebelt Park, which protects neighborhoods from flooding. Turn right on St. George Road. Following the blue blazes, it turns right on Hitchcock Avenue, then left on Mace Street. In one more block, you return to where you started.

For information, or to protect the Amundsen Trailway, contact:
- Coalition for Amundsen Trailway,
- Protectors of Pine Oak Woods   see addresses
- Greenbelt Park   in appendix
- Jacques Marchais Museum of Tibetan Art

BUCKS HOLLOW AND THE
HAUNTING HILL OF HEYERDAHL

Hike up the haunting hill of Heyerdahl, where vine-covered ruins and ghostly legends add a special intrigue. Walk a wild valley, one of the most remote places in the five boroughs. Watch for wildflowers and unusual trees, some of the rarest in New York City.

Distance: 3.2 miles round trip

Level of Difficulty: easy, except a steep, but short, climb up one hill

Things to Bring: a fascination with legends; bug and tick protection, plastic bags for picking up litter, camera, tree and flower guides. Know your poison ivy (occasional here).

Scenic Delights:
The Haunting Hill of Heyerdahl Walk up the spooky front steps of ancient ruins and you'll be greeted with scraggly trees growing out of a collapsed floor, while tangles of vines crawl chaotically across tumbled, decaying walls. This is the old homestead of Mr. Heyerdahl, perched atop a 241-foot hill and overlooking the second-wildest valley in New York City.

From the Colonial era, there is the legend of the ghostly apparition of a young woman in a petticoat riding the horse trails on moonlit nights around Heyerdahl Hill.

The paths of this densely wooded hill are also rumored to have been used by patriotic Revolutionary War spies as escape routes on their way from Richmond Town to Willowbrook's former Christopher House (now located in Historic Richmond Town). Afterward, they ferried across the Kill Van Kull to Continental Army units in New Jersey.

Mr. Heyerdahl struggled to establish wine grape vineyards and orchards on his hill, but he sure didn't pick the right place. The shallow soils were formed out of serpentine bedrock (exposed along many paths here), notorious for its infertility.

Bucks Hollow One-hundred thirty feet below Heyerdahl Hill is Bucks Hollow, a wild sheltered valley interspersed with small swampy areas. Bucks Hollow and Heyerdahl Hill are the 220-acre northern part of Latourette Park. Together, they form the second wildest upland location in the five boroughs, 1,700 feet from the nearest road or home.

Rare Trees and Wildflowers Because it has been undisturbed for so long, many rare plants survive. Staten Island has one of

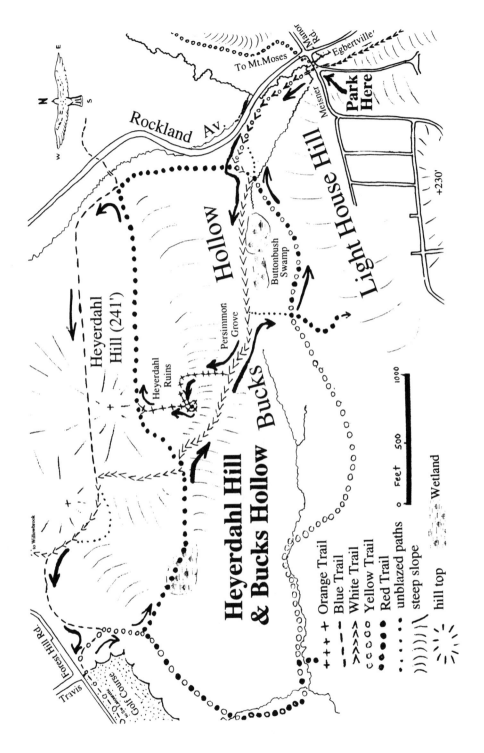

Heyerdahl Hill & Bucks Hollow

Bucks Hollow

N

To Mt.Moses

Egbertville

Manor Rd.

Meisner

Park Here

+230'

Rockland Av.

Light House Hill

Hollow

Buttonbush Swamp

Persimmon Grove

Heyerdahl Hill (241')

Heyerdahl Ruins

Bucks

to Willowbrook

Forest Hill Rd.

Travis

Golf Course

Legend:
+ + + Orange Trail
- - - Blue Trail
>>> White Trail
ccooo Yellow Trail
●●●● Red Trail
••••• unblazed paths
))))) steep slope
☀ hill top
Wetland

Feet 500 1000

America's northernmost groves of wild persimmon trees, and the largest of these is in Bucks Hollow. Persimmons ripen in late autumn and yield edible, orange, plum-sized fruit.

Other rare wildflowers in Bucks Hollow are maidenhair and rattlesnake ferns, soapwort gentian, bloodroot and false mitrewort. Heyerdahl Hill still has small patches of little bluestem prairie, slowly being taken over by woody growth because decades of vandals' arson fires were stopped in the 1980s.

Refuge for Wildlife Because Bucks Hollow is nestled between hills, it is such a good shelter that some wildlife choose not to migrate south for winter. Strikingly colored pheasants often cackle nearby. Redtail hawks soar above, while yellow-breasted chat, flickers, chickadees and warblers call and twitter in the trees.

How to Get There:

By Bus: Take the S54 or 57 to the intersection of Rockland Avenue and Manor Road. Walk 100 feet up Meisner Avenue.

By Car: From S.I. Expressway, exit at Todt Hill Road/Slosson Ave. exit. Coming from the west, turn right off the ramp and then right again on Schmidts Lane which ends at Manor Road. Turn left on Manor Road. Coming from the east, the Service Road will lead you to Manor Road. Turn left on Manor.

Drive south on Manor until it ends at Rockland Avenue. Cross Rockland onto Meisner Avenue and park immediately on your right.

Standing on Meisner Avenue *facing toward Rockland Avenue*, the foot trail begins on your left, next to the stream. Take this white- and yellow-blazed trail into the woods. Cross a foot bridge. For a while, the bird chatter tries to compete with the Rockland Avenue traffic drone. *At the first fork in the trail, you pass through a complex intertwining of trails -- you just **follow white blazes**:* (At the first intersection, pass an unmarked path on the left. At the second trail junction,the Red Trail joins the White Trail from the right. At the third intersection, the Red and Yellow Trails cut off to the left.) **You continue straight ahead on the White Trail.**

Now in the deep woods, bird twitter is almost the only sound. You pass the bird haven, Buttonbush Swamp, barely detectable to the left. This is a good place for the rare wood frog and other frogs in spring. Watch for **persimmon trees**, recognized by their bark with neat vertical rows of little cork-like knobs.

Pass an unblazed side path on the left. Now watch for the Orange Trail on the right and turn onto it (don't follow the White Trail). Climb steeply 60 feet up **Heyerdahl Hill**. Note the fragrant bayberry along the way. At the top, turn left. The trail winds its way, and in a moment, you are at the steps of Mr. **Heyerdahl's home**.

I hope you brought a cake or housewarming gift before you greet Mr. Heyerdahl. Just walk up the steps, knock on his door, and wait patiently .... very patiently. Of course, I'm just kidding; there's no longer a door or a home, just ruins. But whether you believe in ghosts or not, this is an eerie place. Carefully examine the way the walls have fallen, the way Nature has almost reclaimed this site. When the author was a kid, there was a well hole at the edge of the bluff somewhere in front of the steps -- I wonder if it is still there!

On the front doorsteps of the ruins of Heyerdahl's home. Is anybody home?

Mr. Heyerdahl's front stoop is a great place to eat lunch. Before you leave, please pick up litter, including that left by others. After all, you wouldn't want to displease Heyerdahl's ghost!

Leave the ruins and continue on the Orange Trail. Moments later, it passes through an old prairie meadow. At the fork, make a right (this is the not-so-well-blazed Red Trail).

The Red Trail slowly descends the hill through young scrubby forest. Only ten years ago, this was a large prairie and was kept open by vandals who burned it each year. At the next trail junction, you meet the Blue Trail. (If you go straight, Rockland Avenue and a centuries-old mill race are just ahead.)

Turn left on the Blue Trail. The Blue Trail traverses uphill through upland forest and crosses the flat top of the hill. You are now 130 feet higher than where you started. You are near the long-lost horse path associated with the moonlight rides of the petticoated ghost rider (were those muffled hoof beats you just heard!?).

At the next trail junction, the White Trail joins the Blue Trail from the left. In a few minutes, the White Trail cuts off to the right again. You remain on the Blue Trail. Soon you may begin to hear traffic noise as you near Forest Hill Road. Watch for a right turn of the Blue Trail (where it also joined by the Yellow Trail). The Blue and Yellow Trail emerges onto the end of the 12th hole of Latourette Golf Course. Walk immediately to the right and you reach Forest Hill Road, opposite Travis Avenue.

This ends this suggested hike. (If you wish, you can continue the Blue and Yellow Trail as it follows along the golf course and heads south to Southwest Latourette's woods (see page 89)).

Return on the trail you came in on. At the first trail junction, turn left on the Blue Trail. Follow it until the next *right* turn, to return a different way. Take this right onto the White Trail. It will descend Heyerdahl Hill (crossing the Red Trail intersection) and bottom out in Bucks Hollow.

Pass a side path on the right, walk through the persimmon grove and later pass two trail intersections. **Always take the White Trail.** You will cross a bridge and return to Meisner Avenue.

For information, or to help protect Bucks Hollow, contact:

- Protectors of Pine Oak Woods   see addresses
- Greenbelt Park   in appendix
- Urban Trail Club (to assist in trail blazing)

Credit: James Rossi

Bluestem prairie (1970s) at Bucks Hollow, now mostly replaced by trees

SOUTHWEST LATOURETTE AND HISTORIC RICHMOND TOWN: A STEP BACK INTO THE PAST

Step back a century or two in New York City's only historic village. Stroll down a 19th century country lane. See America's oldest surviving elementary school. Enjoy the beauty of bluff, woods, prairie and marsh at the southern tip of the Greenbelt. Admire how a once-defaced landscape has been returned to beauty.

Distance: 2.7 miles round trip

Level of Difficulty: Easy

Things to Bring: a fascination with history; bug repellent, camera, plastic bags to pick up trail litter. Know your poison ivy (occasional to common here).

Scenic Delights:

Step Back Into the Past! Walk into the misty past down Old Mill Road, still the same old-fashioned country lane it was a century ago (complete with genuine 19th century-style muddy potholes). You will enter a landscape reminiscent of Staten Island as it appeared in the early 1800s (minus a few grist mills, orchards and sheep!). At the entrance to Old Mill Road is St. Andrews Church, looking as if time has stood still, with its old spires and a cemetery with gravestones going back to the late 1700s. Stroll through Historic Richmond Town, New York City's only historic country village.

Historic Richmond Town   See old-time Staten Island in a picturesque village that brings up the question, "Can this really be New York City?" You can see thirty historic buildings, with a dozen open to the public. The oldest elementary school in the U.S. is here, **Voorlezer's House**, built in 1695. The 1700 **Treasure House** was named after the cache of gold coins reputed to have been discovered in 1860 hidden in the walls. Here is a sampling of a few more sites:

• the 1720 **Christopher House**, rumored to have been used to hide Revolutionary War patriot spies who snuck across Bucks Hollow (see page 84).

• the 1670 **Britton Cottage**, relocated from the foot of New Dorp Lane, was possibly Staten Island's first government building. It was also the home of Nathaniel Lord Britton, one of Staten Island's great naturalists (see page 14).

• the 1740 **Guyon-Lake-Tysen House**, a farmhouse with remarkable interior woodwork.

• the 1848 **Historical Museum** showcasing Staten Island's entire history. Admission $4 adults, $2.50 seniors and children 6-18, group rates and tours available, 718-351-1611.

• **Church of St. Andrew** (1872), while not formally part of Historic Richmond Town, is an integral and classical part of its setting. The still-active congregation is located at the foot of Old Mill Road, where the natural part of Latourette Park begins. The church and its highly photogenic ancient graveyard present an outstanding scene. The church is not routinely open to visitors. To find out when it is open, contact St. Andrew's Episcopal Church, 40 Old Mill Road, S.I. 10306, 718-351-0900.

Historic Richmond Town was initiated in the 1930s by the Staten Island Historical Society and formally established in 1958 as a partnership with the City of New York. The 100-acre site is part of Latourette Park. The buildings are open year-round, Wed.-Sun. 1-5 pm, extended hours in summer during Living History Season. **The best way to see it is by guided tour.** Allow one and one-half to two hours for the guided tour (and add 45 to 90 minutes if you also see the Historical Museum). For schedules of tours, and for outdoor demonstrations of trades, crafts and traditional activities and celebrations, call 718-351-1611.

Latourette Park The 540-acre Latourette park is comprised of five sections, Southwest Latourette (open woods, prairie and bluffs), Richmond Creek (tidal estuary and marsh), Latourette Golf Course (the middle section), Bucks Hollow-Heyerdahl Hill (wilder mature forest on hills and vales), and Historic Richmond Town.

This is also the southern tip of the Greenbelt. From the meandering curves of Richmond Creek, the Greenbelt extends nearly six miles to the north end of Clove Lakes Park. From Southwest Latourette, you can hike almost entirely through forest on more than 35 miles of public blazed and unblazed trails. The tidal marsh part of the Greenbelt includes the canoeable Richmond Creek estuary and Main Creek (through Davis Refuge -- see page 29).

The Latourette family first settled on this land in the 1690s. In 1777, the British built a fort on the highest hill (now called Fort Hill), where they protected Richmond Town. On this strategic lookout, the British Army could see uninterrupted views of the island, the Atlantic coast and the Arthur Kill.

Southwest Latourette is a wonderful example of how the City parks department restored a defaced land and returned it to beauty. After 200 years of abuse and scarring, the Parks Department created a massive restoration project, still in progress. Look at the sad history of this ancient landscape:

Between the late 1600s and the mid-1800s, all the forest was cut down and turned into grazing meadow and farmland. The steep sandy soils started to erode. After World War I, a large sand mining pit was gouged out of the bluff. In the early 1930s, topsoil was stripped off the bluff top and used to construct Clove Lakes Park and Latourette Golf Course. Between 1948 and the 1960s, the southwest end of the park near Richmond Avenue was covered by a 55-acre garbage dump. From the 1950s to the mid-1980s, Latourette's hills and meadows were used by car thieves and wild groups of youths to junk hundreds of stolen cars. Meanwhile, midnight dumpers illegally disposed of thousands of tires. "Joy riders" and motorcyclists raced their vehicles up and down the steepest slopes, gouging the land with erosion gullies and keeping the land barren of vegetation. Arsonists regularly set the woods and meadows on fire.

In the 1980s, Greenbelt Park staff started the restoration project. On parts of the garbage dump, a baseball field and model airplane field were created. Vehicle access to Southwest Latourette was blocked off to prevent disposal of stolen cars and dumping. Almost 240 junked cars and 2,000 tires were hauled out! Large amounts of undesirable foreign invading weed growth was removed and replaced by more than 20,000 native trees and shrubs. A new improved route for the Blue Trail is now being built.

The result: a friendly landscape of woods and meadow, with views unblighted by junked cars and dumping.

How to Get There:

By Bus: Take the S74 to Richmond Town. Exit at Richmond Road and Court Place. Walk uphill on Court Place to the Court House Visitor Center.

By Car: Coming from the east on the S.I. Expressway, exit at Richmond Road-Clove Road exit. From the exit ramp, proceed to the second light and turn left onto Richmond Road. About five miles ahead, turn left onto St. Patricks Place. Follow signs to Richmond Town parking at the Visitor Center lot off Clarke Avenue. Walk to the Court House Visitor Center entrance.

Begin your walking tour from the Visitor Center. If it is open when you are there, enter the center and pick up a map and information about Historic Richmond Town. Find out when they offer guided tours.

You can do this outing in two ways. You can take this book's brief self-guided tour through Historic Richmond Town and then go on the country walk (two and one-half hours). Or you can do them each on separate days.

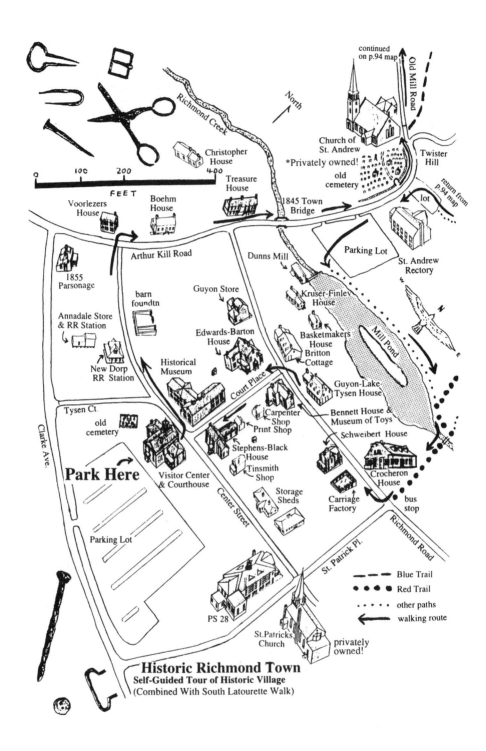

North

Richmond Creek

Christopher
House

Treasure
House

continued
on p.94 map

Old Mill Road

Church of
St. Andrew
*Privately owned!
old
cemetery

Twister
Hill

return from
p.94 map

lot

100   200   400

FEET

Voorlezers
House

Boehm
House

1845 Town
Bridge

Parking Lot

St. Andrew
Rectory

Arthur Kill Road

Dunns Mill

1855
Parsonage

barn
foundtn

Guyon Store

Kruser-Finley
House

Mill Pond

Annadale Store
& RR Station

Edwards-Barton
House

Basketmakers
House
Britton
Cottage

New Dorp
RR Station

Historical
Museum

Guyon-Lake
Tysen House

Court Place

Carpenter
Shop
Print Shop

Bennett House &
Museum of Toys

Tysen Ct.

old
cemetery

Schweibert House

Stephens-Black
House

Clarke Ave.

Park Here

Visitor Center
& Courthouse

Tinsmith
Shop

Crocheron
House

Storage
Sheds

Carriage
Factory

bus
stop

Parking Lot

Center Street

Richmond Road

St. Patrick Pl.

— — — Blue Trail
● ● ● ● Red Trail
· · · · · other paths
←——— walking route

PS 28

St.Patricks
Church

privately
owned!

Historic Richmond Town
Self-Guided Tour of Historic Village
(Combined With South Latourette Walk)

To begin your walk, start on the Center Street side of the **Court House Visitor Center** (other side from the parking lot). Standing with your back to the Court House, look across Center Street on the right side of Court Place to see the 1837 Greek Revival **Stephens-Black House** with the **General Store** attached to it. It was the home of the Stephens and Black families and has 19th century furnishings inside and a Victorian-style flower and fragrance garden in the rear. The General Store is stocked with late-1800s wares. Opposite this site is the 1848 **Historical Museum** with fascinating exhibits, paintings and photos of Staten Island as it was long ago.

To continue, stand along Center Street, with the Historical Museum on your right and the Visitor Center to your left. Now walk forward along Center Street, passing Tysen Court on your left and then the 1888 former **New Dorp Railroad Station** and Depot on your left.

In one block, you reach Arthur Kill Road. Cross the street (**take care -- busy street!**) to the reddish wood building on the other side. This is the 1695 **Voorlezer's House**, the oldest surviving elementary school in the U.S. and a National Historic Landmark. When open, you can see the classrooms and desks of yesteryear (when kids walked long distances and there were no school buses, computers, TVs, Walkmans or Nikes).

Standing in front of Voorlezer's House, look across the street and to your right. This Gothic Revival building is the 1855 **Parsonage**, now a full-service restaurant. Plan to eat there when you finish your walk -- you'll certainly have an appetite of historic proportions! From Voorlezer's House, turn left and walk to the neighboring building, the 1750 **Boehm House**, the former home of a prominent teacher.

Continue walking along Arthur Kill Road. In the distance to your left is the 1720 **Christopher House**, a fieldstone farmhouse that was the reputed meeting place of Revolutionary War patriots. At the intersection of Arthur Kill and Richmond Roads is the 1700 **Treasure House**, first the home of leatherworkers and shoemakers, then a bakery and post office. A cache of gold coins hidden by theBritish during the Revolutionary War was rumored to have be discovered in the walls in 1860.

Continue walking along the road, now called Richmond Hill Road. In a moment, cross Richmond Creek over the only surviving early 19th century **stone arch bridge** in Staten Island. (**Careful -- the stretch of road from here on is narrow and dangerous! Stay off the road at all times!**) After the bridge, you pass the cemetery of St. Andrew's Church on your left, and the church parking lot across

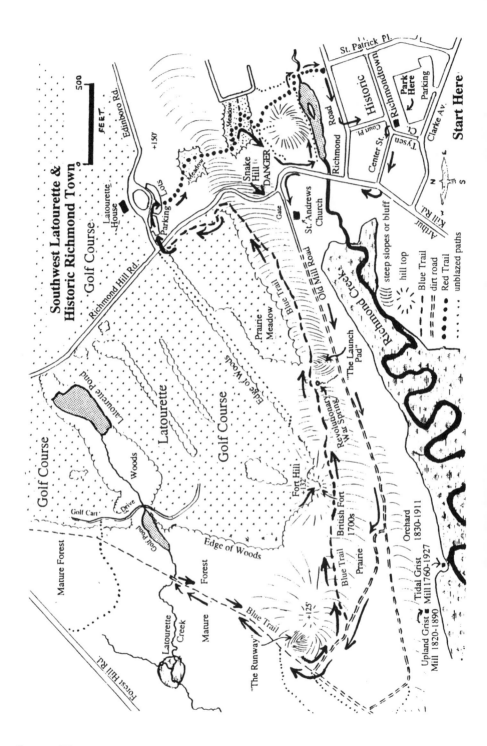

Southwest Latourette &
Historic Richmond Town

the street. The very picturesque **cemetery** has gravestones going back to the 1700s and has graves of prominent islanders including the father of St. Elizabeth Ann Seton.

The ancient cemetery of the Church of St. Andrew

As the road turns sharply cars will zoom around a blind curve, so walk close to the wall! At the narrowest point, **the only safe way is to walk <u>between</u> the wall**

and the steel barrier! DO NOT WALK IN THE STREET -- this is the notorious "Killer Curve" at the bottom of "Snake Hill Road." In 50 feet, you are safely on Old Mill Road.

Walk down **Old Mill Road** and through the gates. Admire the classical Romanesque Revival 1872 **Church of St. Andrew's** (built on the original 1712 foundation). It is generally not open to the public, but take pictures from the road.

As you walk along the dirt Old Mill Road, imagine you are walking into the past. Some country roads back then were just like Old Mill Road!

Notice that a steep, densely wooded bluff rises up to your right. This 100-foot high bluff is the southern tip of the green serpentine backbone ridge that is unique to Staten Island (p.42). Following along the road to the left is a vast area of tall reed grass (*Phragmites*). It screens you from viewing Richmond Creek's marsh and estuary. Hidden out there is a wonderful canoe trip along a winding creek and a wildlife oasis.

Stop when Old Mill Road comes to a fork. A fruit orchard was planted here between 1838 and 1911. Hidden in the marsh to your left and a short way ahead are ruins of a tidal grist mill (1760-1927) and a freshwater grist mill (1820s -1890).

Now take the right fork. As you walk, look up to your right. Notice how the woods here are very open, with bare soil patches and prairie meadow. While attractive now, this is the area that was scarred first by a sand mine pit, then soil stripping, then decades of erosion by joy riders, motorcycles, arson fires and massive dumping.

A memorable walk into the past down Old Mill Road, Latourette Park

Look for newly planted trees. This land is now healing!

The rutted road gradually goes uphill. Watch carefully for the **first trail on the right** (blue-blazed). **Be sure to remember this trail intersection -- you will be returning here on your way back!**

As you continue, the dirt road intersects with another dirt road. *Turn right.* at this four-way intersection. This is the original Forest Hill Road, still looking much as it did in the 1800s (minus the stagecoaches). As this blue-blazed woods road takes you into mature forest, compare it to the "modern" Forest Hill Road a short distance away -- congested with long lines of cars on their way to the mall.

Look for a very steep hill on your right with a shallow ravine running up it. This is humorously named "The Runway" because until recently it was the domain of motorcyclists who ripped down it at high speeds.

The Blue Trail soon takes you to a crossing over a **picturesque brook**. Stop here and enjoy its gurgling peacefulness. Inspect it to see the old stone walls that line it, built a long time ago. Seven hundred feet downstream from you are 15-foot high dirt levees, mysteriously stretching for 1100 feet through the now-mature forest. They were built in the 1820s as a dam for a large mill pond.

We suggest you turn back here and return to the Blue Trail referred to previously. (If you were to continue, you would soon come within sight of the Latourette Golf Course, and then finally reach the intersection of Forest Hill Road and Richmond Hill Road.)

On your way back, you pass the steep hill on your left and soon reach another road on the left. Turn left here and **CAREFULLY WATCH FOR THE MUCH NARROWER BLUE-BLAZED TRAIL** within 500 feet on your left.

This is the same Blue Trail that started in Clove Lakes Park, 5.4 miles to the north! The trail gradually climbs through young oak forest. When it levels off, you are now on **Fort Hill, the site of the former British fort** that stood here during the Revolutionary War. There is no view from this area as there once was (although there is an outstanding vista from the knoll of the second golf tee on the south edge of Latourette Golf Course).

This section of the Blue Trail is very new, built in fall 1997. Therefore, portions may be narrow or may be a bit overgrown during the summer until foot traffic clears it permanently. **Be sure to watch for blue blazes to stay on the correct route.**

Soon, you reach an open section along the crest of the bluff, with clear views. Be sure to stop here and turn around to admire the **vista** over Richmond Creek and its vast marsh estuary. The distant views of church steeples and scattered houses reminds you of a country scene in New England, not a borough of New York City!

When you cross a narrow brook channel, this is the outlet of **Revolutionary Spring**. The spring was used for centuries to supply military troops, farmers, and walkers. While it is probably no longer drinkable (because of fertlizer and pesticide use on the golf course), it is one of the few surviving original springs in New York City!

Shortly after crossing the channel of the spring, you reach a steep eroded gully extending all the way down to the bottom of the bluff. This is humorously nicknamed "The Launch Pad" because dozens of stolen cars were careened off the bluff at this point. Their burned, rusting corpses sat at the bottom for decades until their removal (Thank the Lord!) in the 1990s.

The Blue Trail continues to skirt the crest of the bluff. When the trail starts to bend left and up the hill, you can hear and see the "Twister Hill" of Richmond Hill Road below you. You wonder why they haven't closed this dangerous road years ago (it's not even an official city road according to the Highway Department!).

The trail emerges onto a meadow just outside a golf driving range. Carefully watch for scattered blue blazes as the trail skirts the edge of the meadow, parallel to the road. When you reach the golf cart driveway, turn right. You are now at Richmond Hill Road, a hazardous spot! **Cross it very quickly and carefully.**

Now follow these directions carefully! Watch for blue blazes painted on widely separated fence posts or trees. Cross the first parking lot, and walk parallel to the wooden fence. Pass through the narrow spot between the first and second parking lot (notice a blue blaze on a tree), pand enter the second lot. (To your left is the **David Latourette House**, built in 1836, an ideal place to watch sunsets.)

Follow the edge of the woods to the right about 50 steps and w*atch very carefully for a foot path* that enters the woods on your right. (The trail blaze may not be visible yet.) This is where the Red and Blue Trails descend the bluff. The trail opening can be somewhat overgrown in summer. As soon as you enter it, you'll see a large post with red and blue blaze.

The trail descends through woods and enters a small meadow with high grass and goldenrod. Take the trail to the opposite side of the meadow and re-enter woods. It will descend a steep rocky hill. **Watch for overhanging poison ivy and thorny rose branches.** Enter a large meadow and cross it to the large post with red and blue blazes. (The Blue Trail goes left.) Turn right with the red blazes and enter the woods. When the Red Trail goes left, *walk down an unmarked path to the right and always take the right fork.* You soon enter a grassy area beside the St. Andrew's Parish House.

Walk ahead to Richmond Hill Road but do not cross it. Turn left and pass the Parish House. Cross the larger parking area diagonally toward **Old Mill Pond**. Enjoy the dozens of ducks and the "old country feeling." You can see three historic buildings across the pond. At the pond edge, follow the path to the left. Re-enter the woods and follow along the creek. *Watch for poison ivy!* In a few minutes, the Red Trail enters from the left. You follow the Trail along the creek until it reaches a concrete bridge (on your right). Take it across Richmond Creek. Two hundred feet ahead, cross a field and the Red Trail ends at Richmond Road.

To get back to the Visitor Center and parking lot, turn right along Richmond Road. The first building on your right is the **Crocheron House**, owned and built by a Manhattan merchant in 1819. Across the street is a partially reconstructed 1858 brick carriage and wagon manufacturing house. The **Guyon-Lake-Tysen House** is the next on your right. Built in 1740, this farmhouse has a remarkable surviving wood panel inside. The 1670 **Britton House** follows next on the right. It is the oldest building in Historic Richmond Town and one of the oldest in the entire city. It may have been Staten Island's first government building. Between 1895 and 1915, it was the home of Nathaniel Lord Britton, one of America's most prominent botanists and naturalists (see page 14).

From the Britton House, turn left, cross Richmond Road and walk up Court Place. On your left is the 1839 Greek Revival

Bennett House, the home of a wealthy shipping merchant. Its upper galleries display early toys and dolls. Opposite Bennett House is the 1869 Gothic Revival **Edwards-Barton House**, the former home of a prominent county government official.

The next two buildings on your left are a reconstruction of an 1830s **carpenter shop** and the 1860 **Eltingville Print Shop**. Notice the **1860 outhouse** behind them!

As you complete your journey, you pass the **Historical Museum, the Stephens-Black House and General Store**, and then reach the Court House Visitor Center at the end of the street. Check out the **museum store** for a souvenir. Consider dining at the **Parsonage Restaurant** on Arthur Kill Road. To return to your car, look for the parking lot located on the other side of the center.

For information, or to support protection of the park, contact:

- S.I. Historical Society (incl. historical re-enactments or to help restore historic structures)
- Protectors of Pine Oak Woods
- Urban Trail Club (to help blaze trails)
- Friends of Clearwater (canoeing on Richmond Creek)
- Greenbelt Park (which manages Latourette Park)

see addresses in appendix

Verrazano Bridge spans both the bay and history at Fort Wadsworth (see next page) --->

FORMIDABLE FORT WADSWORTH:
OPEN TO THE PUBLIC FOR THE FIRST TIME

Tour one of the oldest forts in America, off-limits to the public for 200 years -- until now. Marvel at the monumental size of two standing forts and the remains of several more. Get the eerie feeling of walking through a dark and deep moat with gun slots aimed at you on both sides. View the incredible panorama of the bay, under the shadow of the Verrazano Bridge.

Distance: 1.2 mile round trip

Level of Difficulty: easy, with gradual, moderate climb along the road to return to the top of the bluff

Things to Bring: an appreciation for history and a love of old forts; camera, binoculars

Hours: Open daily, Mon.-Fri., 1-5 PM, Sat.-Sun., 10 AM-5 PM

Scenic Delights:
Fort Wadsworth: Called the "Guardian of the Narrows," the imposing presence of Fort Wadsworth has secured the "Gateway of America" for 200 years. Off-limits to the public (except for a rare special tour), the old part of the military base is now open to public visitation (and this is the first tour guide to describe it!). One of the oldest military installations in the U.S., it is now the city's newest National Park site (as of 1998).

Since the late 1700s, 200-acre Fort Wadsworth has stood poised to defend the harbor of the country's most important city. Because of its formidable firepower and strategic position, no foe ever challenged it. During the last 200 years, no shots were ever fired in actual battle; but now thousands of shots will be fired -- by sightseers' cameras! The commanding **panorama** of the Verrazano-Narrows Bridge, the harbor and the Manhattan skyline is one of the finest in the world.

Fort Wadsworth is actually several fortifications:
Battery Weed: Named after Gen. Stephen Weed, the most impressive of the gun batteries boasted 102 muzzle-loading cannons that could destroy any enemy ship entering the harbor. Built on a site from the 1790s, it was constructed in 1847 and is made of massive granite-cutstone. By 1900, powerful breech-loading guns made it effective in defending New York right through World War II.

Fort Tompkins: Looming 150 feet above the sea, construction was started on this granite and brick fortress in 1814, then reconstructed beginning in 1859. Surrounding it on three sides are impressive deep moats, built to protect from a land attack. The fort was named after Daniel Tompkins, former U.S. vice president and New York governor.

Battery Catlin: This and eleven other Endicott-era batteries are smaller structures that overlook the bay to the north and south of Battery Weed. The current structures were built between 1895 and 1904, although previous batteries existed here as early as 1808.

The Torpedo Building : A large ruin across the access road from Battery Weed, it stored mines (then called "torpedoes") which were transported to Battery Weed along rail tracks.

Gateway National Recreation Area After the Nike missiles became obsolete in 1960, Fort Wadsworth served as a housing and administrative facility. In 1972, Congress passed a law directing that the 226-acre fort complex, if it were ever to be declared "surplus," would have to be transferred to the National Park Service. In 1987, the Army indeed departed the site and in 1994, after a brief use by the U.S. Navy, the military flag was lowered. The "Gateway to the Narrows" now became part of the Gateway National Recreation Area. Other units of Gateway are Brooklyn's Floyd Bennett Field; Queens' Fort Tilden, Riis Park, Jamaica Bay Wildlife Refuge; New Jersey's Sandy Hook; and Staten Island's Great Kills Park (see p. 105), Miller Field and Hoffman and Swinburne islands.

World-Class Panorama The world-famous panorama of New York's harbor "unfurls like a banner" stretching from Coney Island to the southeast to Manhattan's majestic skyline to the north, eight miles away. The Verrazano-Narrows Bridge arcs sweepingly over part of this vista, with Brooklyn's Bay Ridge, the Belt Parkway and Fort Hamilton (still in military use) across the Narrows.

The Giant Beech and Tulip Tree Two very impressive trees, a wide-spreading 271-year-old European beech, planted in 1726, with a 5-foot, 7-inch diameter, and a 150- to 200-year old towering tulip tree with a 4-foot, five-inch diameter. Although this area is off-limits to the public, you can inquire about a guided tour that sometimes takes you to these living historical monuments. Ask the guide if you can walk right up to the trees to appreciate their massiveness.

How to Get There:

By Bus: From the S.I. Ferry, take the S51 to Park entrance on Bay Street.

By Car: Coming from the Verrazano Bridge direction of the S.I. Expressway, take the first exit after the toll (Bay Street). Take Wadsworth or

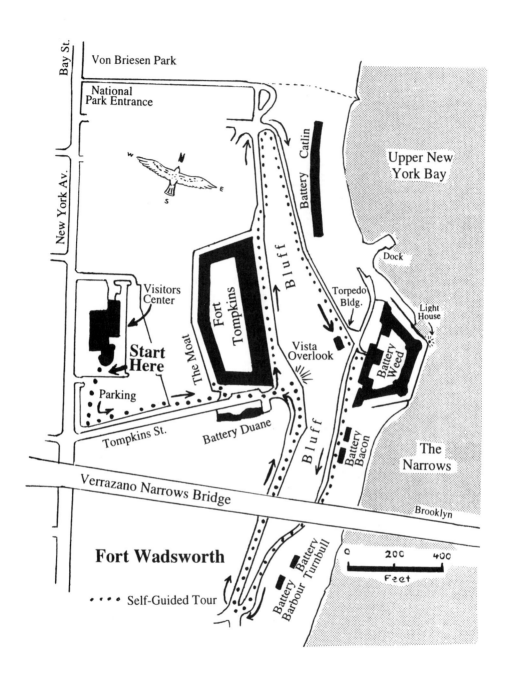

Von Briesen Park

Bay St.

National
Park Entrance

New York Av.

Upper New
York Bay

Battery Catlin

Bluff

W N E S

Dock

Visitors
Center

Fort
Tompkins

Torpedo
Bldg.

Light
House

**Start
Here**

The Moat

Vista
Overlook

Battery
Weed

Parking

Battery Duane

Bluff

Battery
Bacon

The
Narrows

Tompkins St.

Verrazano Narrows Bridge

Brooklyn

Fort Wadsworth

Battery
Barbour

Battery
Turnbull

0   200   400

Feet

• • • • Self-Guided Tour

School Road to Bay Street, make a right and go to the Park entrance. Coming from the west, take the last Expressway exit before the bridge toll (Bay Street). Turn left at the light, follow this road to Bay Street and Park entrance. Follow signs to the **Visitor Center** where you can pick up literature and join a guided tour. Be sure to see the Visitor Center exhibits and film, which depicts the fort's history.

To begin a self-guided tour, start your walk toward the bridge and turn left on Tompkins Street. Your first sight will be the crumbling remnants of **Battery Duane** (built in 1895) on the right and the rising ramparts of **Fort Tompkins** on your left. Sense the history that permeates the air here. Walk between the 30-foot walls of the mysterious moat of Fort Tompkins. Notice the slanting gun slots on both sides of the deep moat. If you were the enemy, you would never make it past the crossfire!

Walk past the Fort's towering walls to the overlook of the bay, where you are presented with the **world-famous panorama**. Scan to your right and see if you can identify the old parachute jump and Ferris wheel of Coney Island directly under the middle of the span of the bridge. At the opposite end of the bridge is the Brooklyn VA Hospital, and Fort Hamilton, still an active military base, identified by the large flag to the right of the bridge towers. Scan to the left along Bay Ridge and then to the jagged skyline of Manhattan. This is also a great birding spot!

On your left is the entrance door into Fort Tompkins, open only by guided tour. Look at the giant doors, which are made of bald cypress wood shipped from the deep South.

This suggested self-guided tour turns left from the overlook and passes the front of Fort Tompkins (the guided tour takes you into the fort!). After the fort, take the first right which gradually descends the imposing bluff. On the way down, watch for the ruins of Battery Catlin to your left.

At the bottom is the ruin of the **Torpedo Building** across from the fort. The rails you cross carried the artillery into the fort. Look up the high bluff at the imposing Fort Tompkins. No wonder they called it impregnable!

Across from the Torpedo Building is the massive **Battery Weed**, "built to last for ages." (A visit inside it is part of the guided tour.) After observing the dense growth of trees and weeds on and between the fortifications, you may think Battery "Weed" is well named (it was actually named after Brig. General Stephen Weed who was killed in the Civil War's Battle of Gettysburg).

As you walk the road back up the hill, you pass the ruin of **Battery Bacon**. The road goes under the ever-dominant bridge, with its perpetual roar of traffic. After the bridge, the road passes more rem-

Soldiers re-enacting history at Fort Wadsworth

nants of former batteries -- **Battery Barbour** and **Battery Turnbull**. The road then makes a sharp turn to the left and soon passes back under the bridge. You arrive at Fort Tompkins again. Turn left and follow Tompkins Street back to the Visitor Center.

For information, including historical reenactments, contact:

- Fort Wadsworth Visitor Center, 718-354-4500
- Gateway National Recreation Area Hdqrs (see address in appendix)
- Daniel Tompkins Historical Society, Box 40121, S.I., NY 10304
- Fort Hamilton Historical Society , 230 Fort Hamilton Pkwy, Brooklyn, NY 11252, 718-630-4349 (for history questions)

Land's end: a scene of solitude at the tip of Crooke's Point, Great Kills (see next page) ---->

GREAT KILLS: THE GATEWAY TO LAND'S END

Stroll a beautiful beach with a classic vista. Walk a long peninsula to the "land's end." Savor the sea breeze, and at times, the solitude. Experience the Great Monarch Butterfly Migration. Sight unusual waterbirds. Enjoy swimming, biking, fishing, ranger-guided tours and other outdoor activities at this unit of Gateway National Recreation Area.

Distance: Longer Option - 5 mile loop; Short Option - 1.5 mile loop

Level of Difficulty: Easy

Things to Bring: Tick protection, binoculars, camera, plastic bags for litter pickup, bird and flower guides. Optional: fishing gear, swim suit, sun blocker. Know your poison ivy.

Scenic Delights:
Crooke's Point You really feel as if you've reached "land's end" when you walk to the tip of this narrow one-mile long sand peninsula or "spit." Crooke's Point was at one time a long sand *island* that got detached from the mainland by storms and erosion. In the early 1900s, it was permanently attached and stabilized and Great Kills harbor was formed.

> I want ... solitude and silence, such as all Wall Street cannot buy ... I must live along the beach, on the southern shore, which looks directly out to sea, and see what that great parade of water means, that dashes and roars ... as long as I have lived.
>
> *Naturalist Henry Thoreau, describing Staten Island's shore in 1843*

The Classic Vista From Crooke's Point, on a clear day, you can see up to 20 miles, from the Empire State Building to Long Island's Rockaway to New Jersey's Sandy Hook (illustrated on p.12).
The Monarch Butterfly Migration Great Kills is one of the important landing sites for the great migration of the monarch butterfly. Every late September, millions take off from points north and fly to their ancestral home in tropical Mexico. The monarch is a large and stunningly bright orange butterfly with black lattice lines that create a stained glass effect. The park rangers hold guided tours to see the monarchs flocking. Watch for the butterflies resting on tree trunks. Under ideal conditions, you may see dozens. To see the butterflies, call 718-761-7496 for Protectors Monarch outings.
The Wildlife Great Kills is great for shorebirds of all kinds, especially during their migration in May and September (also the

During the great migration, the monarch butterlies land on kids, too!

month for tree swallows). Shorebirds are best seen at the mud flats on the northern beach of the park. Watch for ducks, geese, gulls and terns offshore or in the yacht harbor. Sightings include uncommon horned lark in grass, the unusual longspurs and snow buntings in winter, and exquisite black-crowned night herons, great blue herons and great egrets in marshy areas. Watch for short-eared owls in winter. On the shore, search for fascinating shells such as surf, mud and hard shell clams, blue and ribbed mussel, scallop, periwinkle and crabs. You may see shells best after storms and at low tide.

 The Beach From the beach, visitors savor the sun, the sand, the sea wind, the soothing swoosh of the surf, the seabirds and the sea shells (boy -- that's a lot of S-words!). The park's 1.5-mile beach along Raritan Bay is part of the five-mile long continuous beach starting at South Beach. The beach center was just rebuilt in 1997 (wave erosion washed the 1952 structure into the sea). Other facilities are a marina, ball fields, model airplane fields, picnicking, walking, jogging and biking paths, and jetties for fishing.

oyste

mud baske
snail

 Gateway National Recreation Area The importance of the New York City metro area's coastal resources was recognized in 1972, when nine sites were designated as Gateway National Recreation Area: Staten Island's Fort Wadsworth, Miller Field, two offshore islands, and Great Kills Park; Jamaica Bay Wildlife Refuge,

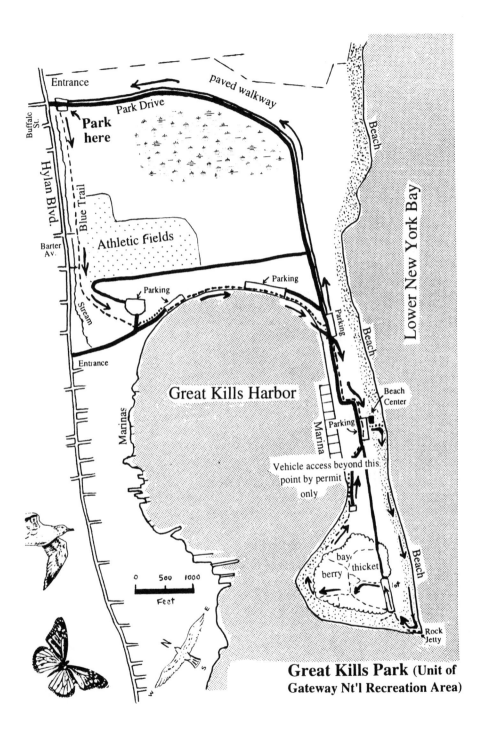

Entrance

paved walkway

Park Drive

Buffalo St.

Park here

Hylan Blvd.

Blue Trail

Barter Av.

Athletic Fields

Stream

Parking

Parking

Entrance

Great Kills Harbor

Marinas

Marina

Parking

Beach Center

Vehicle access beyond this point by permit only

bayberry thicket

Beach

Lower New York Bay

Beach

Beach

Rock Jetty

0 500 1000

Feet

N E S W

Great Kills Park (Unit of **Gateway Nt'l Recreation Area**)

Floyd Bennett Field, the Queens Breezy Point Unit (Jacob Riis Park and Fort Tilden); and New Jersey's Sandy Hook. That means that Staten Island has its own *National* Park lands.

How to Get To Great Kills Park:

By S.I. Rapid Transit: Get off at Bay Terrace Station. Walk south on Bay Terrace, turn left at Hylan Blvd., go seven blocks to park entrance on right.

By Bus: Take the S78 from ferry or the S79 from Bay Ridge (Brooklyn) to Great Kills Park entrance.

By Car: From S.I. Expressway, exit at Hylan Blvd. Take Hylan south 4.75 miles to entrance of park. *As soon as you turn into the park entrance road,* pull off into the **right-hand** parking lot.

Look for the Blue Dot Trail at the corner of the parking lot closest to Hylan Blvd. **Do not take the wide, gated trail that has a sign "Do Not Enter."** Instead, look for a blue dot blaze on a wood post at the edge of the lawn to the right. This marks a *narrow* trail.

Follow the Blue Dot Trail through meadow and thicket. Enter young woods that parallel the deep ravine of a canal. You can hear Hylan Boulevard's traffic at times.

In 0.4 mile, pass a trail that connects to Hylan, opposite Bartow Street. You continue to pass behind various ball fields. Then the trail suddenly bears left, leaves the woods, crosses a meadow and ends up on a dirt road intersection within sight of **Great Kills Harbor**. You have now walked 0.7 mile.

Walk to the edge of the harbor and follow it *to the left. Walk quietly, with your binoculars ready.* You may see flotillas of beautiful **waterbirds**, or a graceful, long-legged heron or egret.

moon snail

As you reach the other side of the harbor, cross the park road to the new beach center. Walk to the **beach** and turn right. As you follow the beach to the end of Crooke's Point, enjoy the **panorama** (illustrated on p. 14). Far to the left over the trees are the Verrazano Bridge and Manhattan skyline, including the World Trade Center. To the right is Coney Island, Long Island's Rockaway, New Jersey's Sandy Hook (a unit of Gateway National Recreation Area) and the Atlantic Highlands. Observe the interesting habits of the wildlife (especially those human creatures!). Look for sea shells, crabs, birds, and driftwood.

mud clam

slipper shell

Show you care for the environment by picking up cans, bottles and other litter, including tangled fishing line that can choke birds. (I think it's a reasonable goal to haul out a full plastic bag of litter on each beach walk.)

hard shell clam

A mile south of the beach center, you reach the **rock jetty** at the end of the point. You are at "land's end." Walk onto the jetty and look at the boulders. Some are covered with shiny flecks. These are mica schist. This tough rock was possibly removed from 1000 feet below the bay during the building of the city's huge water tunnel.

Leave the jetty and continue walking down the beach a hundred feet or so. Look carefully to your right across the sand to see a fence or cars. Head toward this to reach a parking lot (only for vehicles with fishing or other special permits). As you enter the lot, you pass the first trail opening into the thicket on your left. Several hundred feet further, enter the second trail opening (marked by three orange dots and two wooden posts). (**You should be dressed for tick protection here**; see page 4 for details.)

Jap. honey suckle

Take the path into the thicket, which is the place to see bayberry and rare plants. **Follow the orange-blazed trail.** Along the path, notice the bayberry, whose leaves have the scent of (you guessed it) bayberry candles. Other plants along the path are dwarf sumac (edible, not poisonous), black cherry, Japanese honeysuckle, blue stem grass, and of course, poison ivy. A rare plant is beach heather (*Hudsonia*), a downy, evergreen, low-growing beach shrub.

The trail exits onto the harbor side of the peninsula. Follow the harbor edge to the right. When you reach a lone tree, look across the harbor. Observe in the distance a long wooded hill with a radio tower. This is Todt Hill, the highest point on the Atlantic seaboard, south of Maine (see p. 42). On a clear day, to the right of the hill, you can also see the World Trade Center and the Verrazano Bridge.

dwarf sumac

Continue along the harbor edge until a boat marina forces you onto the park road. Follow it past the beach center. At the opposite end of the harbor, you have two choices for your return trip. You can either return the same way you came (follow the harbor edge to the Blue Dot Trail), or follow the wide paved multi-use trail that parallels the park drive back to your parking lot.

Alternate Short Option (round trip of 1.2 miles):

Drive your car 1.5 miles down the park entrance road until the *very last* parking lot. *Note that cars are not permitted any further without a special permit.* Walk to the beach. Turn right and stroll to the jetty at the end of Crooke's Point. Follow the above instructions from Crooke's Point and you will loop back to your car.

For information or to help protect Great Kills, contact:
- Gateway National Recreation Area   see addresses
- Friends of Gateway Parks, 212-513-7555   in appendix
- Protectors of Pine Oak Woods

HOW TO FEEL ETERNITY:
THE ANCIENT FOREST OF WOLFE'S POND

This is a rare place, where you can sense "eternity" beneath Staten Island's largest old growth forest. Stroll silently in a seldom-seen ravine past towering 200- to 300-year old trees. Treat yourself to sights of freshwater birds and wildlife, only 70 yards from saltwater wildlife. Picnic, swim or fish along a fine bay beach.

Distance: 1 mile round trip
Level of Difficulty: mostly easy, except for short hill slopes. During springtime high water, the brook may be difficult to cross and parts of the path could be muddy.
Things to Bring: an appreciation for cathedral settings; bug protection, camera, binoculars, bird and tree guides, plastic bags to pick up trail litter; boots for mud in wet periods. Know your poison ivy (occasional here).

Scenic Delights:

The Ancient Forest Secluded in a deep ravine is Staten Island's oldest and largest surviving grove of old-growth forest. Here you can see huge oaks and tulip trees dating back to the early 1800s or older -- living history monuments as significant as Richmond Town. Stand under these monuments and try to sense the eternity of this forest cathedral.

How did this forest survive being cut down as did virtually all other forest on Staten Island? The ravine was too steep to be farmed. While selected cutting of some trees probably occurred in the early centuries, this five-acre tract of old woods always remained in a forested state. Most of the oldest trees are venerable tulip trees, beech, and black, red and white oaks. The largest are stupendous: a 5-foot, 2-inch diameter black oak, and a 4-foot diameter tulip tree.

black oak

Wolfe's Pond Fresh water just yards from the sea! This is what Wolfe's Pond offers. Once a tidal inlet, the 16-acre pond was created when creek silt and tidal sands dammed the inlet, cutting off the salt water. Oystermen once rinsed their daily catch here. Lenape Indians also camped here, collected seafood and left oyster middens.

The Wildlife If you visit the pond on a misty morning or evening, you may be blessed with a memorable scene: six or so white egrets and herons, standing silently, as if frozen in time. You can also sight kingfisher, wood duck and mallard. Cedar waxwings, scarlet tanagers and thrushes are a few of the woodland birds you may see or hear. During the great spring migration, numerous tiny warblers may flutter past you. If you're lucky, rare iridescent and glistening purple martins may flit over the pond in summer.

What makes Wolfe's Pond most unusual is that you can stand on the beach and see saltwater birds, then walk only a couple hundred feet and see freshwater birds. Toward the sea, use binoculars to see bufflehead, cormorant, laughing and herring gulls, and flocks of brant (a short-necked goose) in spring.

The Park The 317-acre Wolfes Pond Park was named after Joel Wolfe who farmed the land near here until 1857. Then the site became a popular spot for summer vacations and 90 shoreline bungalows were built. After the park was purchased in 1929, a political scandal erupted in 1933 when the parks commissioner allowed friends to use the bungalows and block public access to the pond. A lengthy court battle led to removal of all the bungalows.

Besides hiking and wildlife watching, the park offers a half-mile beach, picnicking, fishing, jogging and summer concerts.

Little visited is the section north of Hylan Boulevard, which is just as large as the bay-side portion. Here, Acme Pond, three wetlands and a well-trailed dry oak forest offer scenic and wildlife opportunities.

How to Get There:

By S.I. Rapid Transit: Exit at Prince's Bay Station. Walk south (toward the bay) on Seguine Avenue to Hylan Blvd. Cross the street and turn left. Walk to the park entrance and follow the park road to the last parking lot.

By Bus: From S.I. Ferry, take the S78 to the entrance of the park. Follow the park road to the last parking lot.

By Car: Take the S.I. Expressway to the West Shore Expressway (Rte.440 South). Get off at Bloomingdale Road. At the end of the exit ramp, turn left on Bloomingdale and go about two miles to Amboy Road. Turn left on Amboy and drive 3/4 mile to Seguine Avenue. Make a right and when you reach Hylan Blvd., turn left and drive a half mile to the park entrance. Take the park road to the last lot. Park at the end of the lot, in the corner *away* from the bay.

Walk to this corner of the parking lot. Take the wide foot path toward the pond. Turn right through the woods, with the pond on your left. You enter attractive mature woods. At the next left, take the foot path across the brook by jumping the rocks. (It could be difficult to do this at high water.) Admire the impressive woods.

Take the first left. After passing many **towering trees,** you encounter the **five-foot diameter black oak,** twisted and leaning over the ravine. Make sure to put your hand on the trunk, or hug the tree -- this is the only way to gauge the massiveness of it.

Continue down the foot path. The pond comes into view

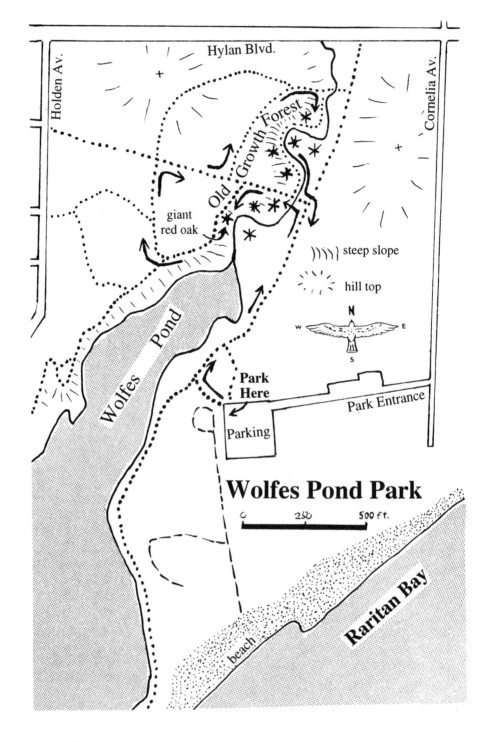

Holden Av.

Hylan Blvd.

Cornelia Av.

Old Growth Forest

giant
red oak

)))) steep slope

`'` hill top

N
W E
S

**Park
Here**

Park Entrance

Parking

Wolfes Pond

Wolfes Pond Park

0   250   500 ft.

beach

Raritan Bay

through the trees. At the first foot path on the right, turn. Stay right at the next fork. After you slowly climb a bit, you reach a four-way trail junction. Turn right and head down hill, but make sure to turn left at the next foot path. (If you reach the brook, you passed it.) As the foot path winds through the woods, look for mushrooms in late summer and fall. The foot path descends, is joined by another foot path and stops at the brook.

Don't cross the creek. Turn right and follow the edge of the brook (there is no path for the first 20 feet). You have entered the **steepest part of the ravine**, with banks rising 50 feet above you.

Continue following the edge of the brook and it becomes a path again. Stand in awe at the **towering tulip** trees. Sit down here awhile and close your eyes. Sense the ancientness of this place -- it is much like it was before European settlers. Try to feel the stillness of time, the eternity. Realize these sentinel trees have stood witness here to storm and drought, and all the crazy machinations of mankind.

tulip tree

Continue walking through the ravine. When you reach the next path, turn left and cross the brook. Turn right and you return to the parking lot. With your forest tour completed, you can now choose to visit the beach or stroll along the pond.

For information or to help protect the park, contact:
- Protectors of Pine Oak Woods
- NY City Parks & Recreation

see addresses in appendix

Credit: Harry Madden

Contemplating under the Great Oak, Wolfes Pond Park

white oak

THE DRAMATIC BLUFFS OF MOUNT LORETTO

Stand atop the highest oceanside cliff in New York State, the dramatic bluffs of Mt. Loretto. Stroll a gentle country lane across a vast, sweeping meadow. Admire the classic landscape, New York City's last remnant of the pastoral era of the 1890s. Walk further back into time along a beach beneath towering bluffs created when dinosaurs roamed the Earth. Admire this wildlife oasis, a place to see large wading birds, geese, osprey and unusual songbirds.

Distance: 1.8 miles round trip

Difficulty: Easy, except a short climb up a path from the beach.

Things to bring: binoculars and bird book, bug repellent, plastic trash bags, small backpack (to collect unusual rocks or sea-smoothed bottles), beach blanket. Know your poison ivy.

IMPORTANT: Because it is still privately owned, you must get permission from Mt. Loretto, Stephen Rynn, 718-317-2803 to visit it.

Scenic Delights:

The Bluffs of Mt. Loretto At 85 feet above Prince's Bay, these cliffs are the tallest ocean-facing cliffs in New York State. From their top, they offer one of the finest panoramas in the New York City area, nearly 360 degrees around. From their base, you can collect "Indian Paint Pots," 135 million year-old box-like, hollowed-out rocks. These are formed of a material like cemented red sand, sometimes filled with a deep red powder or clay-like paste. Staten Island's Native Americans, the Lenapes, did indeed use them as sources of face and body paint. In fact, it is possible this bluff is the source of the original Indian (Lenape) name for Staten Island, "Aquehonga," which means "high sandy bluff."

The bluffs have a fascinating geological history. They were formed about 135 million years ago, during the Age of Dinosaurs (Mesozoic Era). As the ancestral Appalachian Mountains eroded, streams carried their grains of mud and sand to the edge of the sea, depositing the layers you see in this cliff face. It is possible that dinosaurs lived nearby, maybe even walked across this muddy surface. Much later, 15,000 years ago, the massive Ice Age glacier shoved this pile of sand, clay and gravel from New Jersey -- where it was created -- to where it is today, a journey of many miles! It also laid down the upper layers you see in the cliff face. After its forcible relocation, it was sculpted by the sea, and now you can look up at the layers of time recorded in its vertical face.

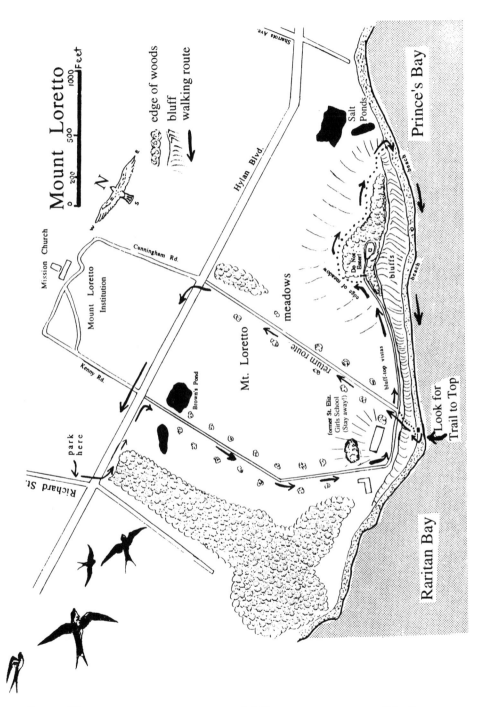

Mount Loretto

edge of woods
bluff
walking route

N

0   200   500   1000 Feet

Mission Church

Mount Loretto Institution

Cunningham Rd.

Hylan Blvd.

Shartela Ave.

Kenny Rd.

Richard St.

park here

Brown's Pond

Mt. Loretto meadows

return route

former St. Eliz. Girls School (Stay away!)

Do Not Enter!

edge of meadow

bluff-top vistas

bluffs

beach

Salt Ponds

beach

Look for Trail to Top

Prince's Bay

Raritan Bay

Mt. Loretto   On your way up to the bluff, you will walk through the last extensive landscape in New York City that preserves the pastoral scenes of the 19th century. From atop the windswept bluff, you can look over 360 acres of vast, tranquil meadow, and country lanes dotted with historic buildings and churches. We owe this rare opportunity to the Mission of the Immaculate Virgin, which has kept its property, appropriately, immaculately unchanged (and immaculately mowed). They also have the generosity to allow visitors to walk the seaside part of the property (145 acres).

Therefore, show your respect by taking only photos, and leaving only footprints! **Do not go near or disturb any building.** Respectful behavior by visitors will ensure continued open access to this jewel of a property.

Father John Drumgoole founded this site as a home for orphans in 1877. Through its doors have passed thousands of children, raised with care and love. Today, you can see the Gothic-style church of Saints Joachim and Ann, a half mile west of the bluff viewpoint. On the bluff top itself is the now unused former St. Elizabeth Girls' School, built in 1893. The Sisters of St. Francis (Archdiocese of NY) now focus on programs for children with developmental disabilities and programs for youth and seniors.

The Panorama   A fabulous panorama, one of the finest in the New York City area, awaits you. Read ahead for a description.

Mt. Loretto and its bluffs overlook Prince's Bay, part of Raritan Bay. The graceful curved shore of this beautiful bay appears much as it did 50 years ago, and even resembles scenes painted by 19th-century painters. The bay was named for a prince who demanded that oysters served to him as an aphrodisiac come from this area.

The Wildlife Oasis   If you like seeing wildlife, you're in the right place! This spot is directly on the Great Atlantic Migratory Bird Flyway. On my last walk to this wildlife oasis, I saw a great blue heron (which stands four feet tall), great egret, the threatened osprey (an eagle relative), Canada geese, glossy ibis, flotillas of seabirds and many others. Three ponds and the cliff-top view over Prince's Bay are the place to see these. The meadow offers views of an uncommon and melodious bird, the bobolink, which has flocked here in May.

How to Get There:

By Car: Take the S.I. Expressway to West Shore Expressway (Rte. 440 South). Exit at Bloomingdale Road. At the end of the exit ramp, turn left on Bloomingdale and go about two miles to Amboy Road. Turn left on Amboy and make an immediate right on Sharrott Avenue. Drive a half mile to Hylan Blvd. Turn right, and you will soon pass between the immaculate meadows of Mt.

Loretto. Turn onto the first street (Richard Avenue) on the right past the meadows. Park close to Hylan Blvd.

Walk across Hylan, and turn left. About 400 feet later, turn right onto a gated country road. You are now on Mt. Loretto's property. **STAY AWAY FROM ALL BUILDINGS AND DISTURB NOTHING!**

Almost immediately, you'll see **Brown's Pond** on your left, and to your right, another pond further off. Look for water birds of all kinds -- this is an oasis!

After your flirt with feathered friends, continue walking up the lane to the top of the hill. On your left is the great building of the former St. Elizabeth Girls' School, dating from 1893. Staying away from the building, continue walking on the lane with the seaward side **always to your right**. Follow the lane along the windswept crest as it rises higher and higher. Admire the vista across the huge lawns.

Where the road comes close to the bluff, walk to its edge and admire the delightful **panorama. Use caution at the edge and hold the hands of children!** From atop the bluff, you can scan nearly 360 degrees. Looking inland, you overlook sweeping meadows, the 19th century pastoral landscape and the historic Mission Church. Further off are church spires of the hamlet of Pleasant Plains and, four miles away, the bridges of New Jersey. To your right is Staten Island's coast heading toward the southernmost point of New York State! Toward the bay, on a clear day, you can see forever -- or 18 miles north to the Manhattan skyline, 14 miles east to Coney Island, and 14 miles southeast to Sandy Hook and the Atlantic Highlands of New Jersey. With binoculars, look for Red Bank Lighthouse and flocks of seabirds floating offshore in the distance.

When the lane reaches a gate in front of a wooded area, DO NOT GO IN! This is private property and off-limits to the public. Instead, just before the gate, turn left and follow a mowed meadow path. Follow it down and around the wooded hilltop, always keeping the edge of the woods **to your right**. It curves right and enters open woods. Watch on your left for a view over the **Salt Ponds** where you can spy more water birds with your binoculars.

When the trail reaches the beach, turn right, toward the bluffs. On the **beach**, you are reminded for the first time that you are in a borough of New York City--litter! Not only have disrespectful visitors left trash, but the flotsam of the metro area floats up here, too. Here's where you can do your part by showing you care for our environment. With your plastic bags, collect cans and bottles (remember kids, many are worth a nickel each) and whatever else is light enough to take back. Fill a bag and you've done a good deed. If everybody does this, the litter will become minimal.

Where the bluff towers its highest over the beach, walk to its base. Look up and admire the sight of the **tallest ocean-facing cliff in New York State**! At an exposed vertical section of cliff, look at its layers. Look for a distinct layer with brown rocks embedded in it about 15 feet up; these are probably Indian Paint Pots. Look along the cliff base for these curious reddish brown hollow rocks (called concretions). If you're lucky, you'll find one with red "paint" powder or clay in it, which the Indians used it as a body paint. Also, look for clay along the cliff bottom. Kids will love sinking their fingers into it, since it is just like real kids' modelling clay.

ark shell

periwinkle

On the beach, notice the little Coast Guard light beacon. Look for surf clams, slipper shells, whelk snails, oysters, blue crabs, horseshoe crabs and many other kinds of sea life. Also search for unusual driftwood or wave-polished glass pieces.

oyster

As you walk this beach, remember that the layered cliff was created when dinosaurs roamed the Earth. Let your mind travel back in time and imagine a dinosaur (the peaceful plant-eating kind!) appearing from around the bend. Staten Island is one of only two places in New York State where you can see rock landscapes created during the Age of Dinosaurs. This site dates from the last third of the Dinosaur Age, the Cretaceous Period, which ran from 135 million to 65 million years ago (a bit before the Verrazano Bridge opened).

ribbed
mussel

Mt. Loretto bluffs, the highest ocean-facing cliff in NY State

Further down the beach, the bluffs will get lower and lower. Watch for the ruins of a large rectangular concrete platform (can you figure out what it once was?). Look for the words "Trail to top" with an arrow painted on the wall. Climb to the left and to the top of the concrete platform. Then follow the rough rocky path into the woods and up the hill. A little further, you reach the bluff top, the country lane, and the Mt. Loretto meadow (it rhymes!).

Notice a lane straight ahead that goes down and crosses the meadow, passing the old Girls' School. Follow this down to Hylan Blvd. At Hylan, turn left and return to your car on Richard Avenue.

Status of Mt. Loretto: The 145 seaside acres of this amazing site are still owned by the NY Archdiocese. Although 40 acres of the shoreline, bluffs and wetlands are zoned as permanent Open Space and protected wetland, the rest of the seaside acreage is not legally protected. Much of the property is still zoned for development and pressure to sell it for development remains a threat. The state, the local community board and a host of national and local citizen groups support its full protection as permanent open space.

In the meantime, the Mission has wisely and graciously kept it undeveloped. All lovers of beauty and Nature owe a debt of gratitude to the Mission for protecting the treasure called Mt. Loretto.

To help protect Mt. Loretto, contact:
• Protectors of Pine Oak Woods (address in Appendix)

Credit: John Prasek

Beauty and solitude and cliffs on the wild beach of Mt. Loretto

WARD'S POINT: HISTORY AND BEAUTY AT THE SOUTHERNMOST TIP OF NEW YORK STATE

Stroll a wild beach and admire the classic vista from the southernmost point in New York State. Capture the Revolutionary War spirit at the 320-year old Conference House, where Ben Franklin and John Adams met a British admiral in 1776 -- the only peace conference held during the war. See two great and historic trees next to the Conference House. Enjoy views from red clay bluffs in New York City's only forest of hackberry trees. Observe flotillas of seabirds and the age-old gathering of horseshoe crabs and monarch butterflies.

Distance: 2 miles round trip

Level of Difficulty: easy beach and woods walk. Only one short, steep descent

Things to Bring: an appreciation of history; tick and bug protection, binoculars, camera, plastic bag to pick up litter, bird and tree guides. Know your poison ivy (grows commonly here).

Scenic Delights:
   Southernmost Point in New York State At Ward's Point, you can stand on the southernmost tip of the State of New York. It is 312 miles to the northern border with Canada and 309 miles to the western tip of the state. Ward's Point is the moderate protrusion of beach about 1800 feet south of Conference House.
   Unusual Geology The north edge of the park is also the southernmost place that the Ice Age glacier reached on the Atlantic coast. It is hard to imagine that a 500-foot thick layer of ice ground its way from northern Canada, stopping at this very place. It crushed and ground up everything in its path, sliding dozens of feet a day. It slowly melted away, leaving Staten Island's rolling landscape pockmarked with kettle hole ponds, conical hills, and a layer of rock debris spread across the land.
   Conference House This is one of the most historic sites in New York City and the U.S. It was here that the only Revolutionary War peace conference was held. Ben Franklin, John Adams and Edward Rutledge rowed from New Jersey to Staten Island and met with Admiral William Lord Howe on September 11, 1776. As John Adams wrote, Howe walked them "between lines of guards of grenadiers, looking as fierce as ten Furies ..., with bayonets fixed." During their three-hour meeting, Howe made it clear he was not in a

position "to consider the Colonies in the light of independent states." Even though they had lost a string of battles including the Battle of Long Island, Adams proclaimed, "I avow my determination never to depart from the idea of independence."

Peace talks having failed, they departed and no subsequent peace conference was ever held again. Howe's secretary bitterly wrote, "They met, they talked, they parted. And now, nothing remains but to fight it out against a set of the most determined Hypocrites and Demagogues, compiled of the Refuse of the Colonies, that ever were permitted to be the Scourge of a Country."

The Conference House, originally known as the Billopp House, was built around 1680. It is the only surviving pre-Revolutionary manor in New York City. It was given to Col. Christopher Billopp, who was a British Loyalist, to emphasize the British Tory presence on Staten Island. Billopp was captured in 1778 by American troops but was released nine months later. Because the Brits lost the war, Billopp was forced to sell his 373 acres and home for 3,730 £ ($5,600) to Samuel Ward, whose children used it as a farm. This is the family for which Wards Point was named. Interestingly, family member George Ward was famous because of his resemblance to George Washington.

After the Ward heirs moved to Michigan in the 1830s, the house was severely neglected, almost to ruin, by a string of owners until a grassroots movement rallied to save it in 1925. The park now totals 226 acres.

Today, you can see its 17th-century working kitchen and period furnishings by guided tour. Remember to observe the Fourth of July fireworks spectacle from the expansive lawn overlooking Raritan Bay. The site also hosts many concerts and events.

Call 718-984-6046 for guided tours. (Open Wed.- Sun., 1-4 pm, March to December, closed January and February; Nominal fee.)

Unique Native History Wards Point was the site of the largest Indian village in New York City and the largest burial ground. The red clay bluffs were once rich in artifacts as old as 6,000 years old. Some of these flint arrowheads and hand axes are in the collections of the S.I. Institute of Arts & Sciences. The local Lenape bands frequently resided at Wards Point until the 1670s. Centuries of gathering oysters left large shell middens (mounds) -- it proves they were seafood lovers par excellence!

Rare Hackberry Forest If all these unique features weren't enough, Wards Point has one of the northernmost hackberry forests on the coast. This relative of the elm is found commonly only to the South. It grows on top of the red clay bluffs overlooking the beach.

Credit: John Prasek

Wild beach at the southernmost tip of NY State, with Wards Point in distance

beach. What makes it even more unusual is that it normally grows on limy (calcium-rich) soils, which are absent from this region. However, centuries of oyster shell heaps have incorporated enough calcium to allow this tree to flourish.

Historic Trees See the two "Great and Historic Trees" at the Conference House. One on the bay side of the house is a 300+ year-old white mulberry. It is one of the first mulberries planted in the New World and possibly the *oldest in America*! It was brought here in an attempt to grow silkworms, which feed on white mulberry. It is about four feet in diameter and all contorted. Protected by a fence, it is in bad shape but still hanging on. See it before it *becomes* history!

The other historic tree is a stately sycamore. When you stand on the driveway looking at the front of the house, it is to your left. Six feet in diameter, it was probably planted in the 1800s. Note its beautiful peeling bark mottled with tan, light and dark green patches.

sycar

The Scenic Vista This classic vista (illustrated on p. 12) has been enjoyed by centuries of Native and Colonial people (including Franklin and Adams) right up to the present. To the right is New Jersey's Perth Amboy across the Arthur Kill. Following to the left, you'll see the mouth of the Raritan River, and the profile of New Jersey's Atlantic Highlands (including the Twin Lighthouse rising 260 feet above the sea). Curving outward is the great sand spit known as Sandy Hook (part of Gateway National Recreation Area), 15 miles away.

The Wildlife   Wards Point is another wildlife lover's delight. With binoculars, birders can spy dozens of kinds of wildlife. Bufflehead appear as black and white dots bobbing in the murky waters. The NY area's largest flotilla of horned grebes overwinter here, along with many gulls, terns and other seabirds.

This beach is still one of the best places to see the extraordinarily ancient **horseshoe crab gathering** in June. These two-foot long primitive creatures have been gathering like this for 300 million years when they first appeared on Earth.

slipper shell

The beach is also an excellent place to observe sea shells including oysters, blue and ribbed mussel, surf and mud clams, hard shell clams, slipper shells, periwinkles and blue crab. If you're lucky, you may see a wentletrap, razor clam or scallop. Note that it is illegal to collect sea shells from the park because they add valuable nutrients to the soil.

blue mussel

Lastly, this is a landing site of the **Great Monarch Butterfly Migration** in late September to early October (see p.105 for details).

wentle-trap

How to Get There:

By S.I. Rapid Transit: Take it to the last station (Tottenville). Walk south on Bentley Street to Amboy Road. Turn right and walk to Satterlee Avenue. Turn left; walk several blocks to the entrance of Conference House park, on the right.

By Bus: Take the S-78 or S-59 to Craig Avenue; walk one block south to Satterlee Avenue. Make a right, walk half a block.

By Car: Take the S.I. Expressway to the West Shore Expressway (Rte. 440) South. Take it almost to the end, following signs to "Outerbridge Exit." As you approach the Outerbridge Crossing*, **take the last exit before the toll. Do not continue onto the Outerbridge or you will be forced into New Jersey!** The exit puts you onto Veterans Road West. Turn right off Veterans onto an overpass, then make a right again onto Boscomb Road. At the end of Boscomb, turn left onto Page Avenue. Drive on Page to Hylan Blvd. Turn right onto Hylan Blvd. and drive to the end. Turn right onto Satterlee and go one block. Park along Satterlee.

white mulberry

Walk down the driveway to Conference House. Look for the **great Sycamore** to the left, standing by itself. Take the tour of the house if possible. When finished, note the **historic mulberry**, surrounded by a fence, on the lawn facing the bay.

Head down across the beautiful rolling lawn to the beach and turn left. Note the 30-foot high red clay bluffs rising to your left. On top of these is the **rare hackberry forest**. In a quarter mile, you'll pass the old partly submerged pilings of a now-washed away dock.

* The Outerbridge Crossing has a bizarre name. It is the *outer*most bridge in NY City and NY State. It was designed by (yes, it's true) Mr. Outerbridge. Therefore, it could correctly be called the "**Outer Outerbridge Bridge**"!

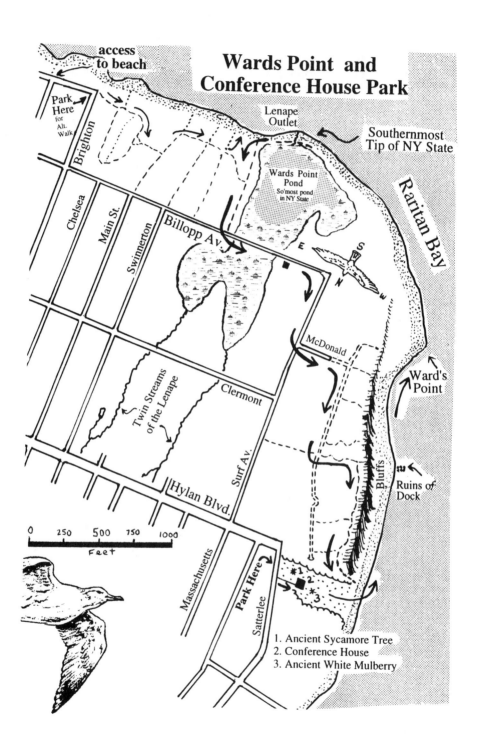

Wards Point and Conference House Park

access to beach

Park Here for Alt. Walk

Brighton

Chelsea

Main St.

Swinnerton

Billopp Av.

Lenape Outlet

Southernmost Tip of NY State

Wards Point Pond
So'most pond in NY State

Raritan Bay

E S N E

McDonald

Clermont

Twin Streams of the Lenape

Surf Av.

Hylan Blvd.

Ward's Point

Bluffs

Ruins of Dock

0 250 500 750 1000
Feet

Massachusetts

Park Here

Satterlee

*1
*2
*3

1. Ancient Sycamore Tree
2. Conference House
3. Ancient White Mulberry

See how many kinds of sea shells and crabs you see along the way! If you are there at low tide, you may see sea lettuce, a bright green leafy, edible seaweed, carpeting the shore. Don't forget to pick up deposit cans and bottles!

The beach curves to the right, reaching a blunt, rounded sandy point a half mile from where you started: **Wards Point**. Admire the **panorama** (illustrated on p.12) and the offshore lighthouse. Also look inland and imagine -- just beyond the trees -- a 500-foot high glacier looming above all, about 15,000 years ago.

Continue walking along the beach. Up to Wards Point, you were walking south. Now the beach curves southeast and then east. About one-third mile past the point, note how the woods and thickets close in on the beach. When you reach a wetland of tall reed (*Phragmites*) grass that comes within 25 feet of the water, you are now standing at the **southernmost point of New York State**. This is also the 4-acre Wards Point Pond, **southernmost pond in the state**, (and in danger of being lost due to development which threatens to cut off its water supply through the Twin Streams of the Lenape).

Walk just past the small stream outlet that crosses the sand. If the stream is too wide at times of high water, look for a wide path to your left in the tall reed grass and take a small wood plank bridge over the creek.

Walk *just past* this wetland. *When it ends, immediately look for a foot path* heading away from the beach. Take this foot path into the young woods of sassafras, black cherry, oak, Japanese honeysuckle (watch for poison ivy). Follow it straight ahead, passing a side foot path, and you will reach Billopp Avenue.

Turn left on the road. You will pass a lone house and then the road makes a sharp right onto Surf Avenue. Follow Surf Avenue until it reaches McDonald Street, a dead-end. Turn left on McDonald. At its end, a foot path begins. **From here on, follow these directions exactly!** Turn right at the first trail junction. Continue straight 750 feet, ignoring two side foot paths on your left that take you downhill back to the beach. At the third foot path on the left, turn. If you do not reach the top of a very steep bluff within 100 feet, you turned off prematurely.

Now turn right, following the narrow foot path along the margin of the cliff-top (which is to your left). You are now in the **rare hackberry woods**. Watch for the leaves of this tree (*and avoid overhanging poison ivy*). At one or two spots, make sure to take a side foot path to a lookout over the bay (**take safety precautions!**). At another spot, you may pass a rope dangling down the cliff for the recreation of those without acrophobia.

hackberry

The bluff path finally descends steeply and you will end up back on the beach and next to the vast lawn, with the Conference House up the slope.

Alternate Walking Route:
You can choose to begin your walk from the opposite end of the park. Ten blocks from the end of Hylan Blvd., turn right off Hylan onto Brighton St. Drive three blocks to its end. Look for a meadow path off the right side of the dead-end. **The foot paths are not marked, so you should use the map.** The general pattern is that side foot paths to the left take you to the beach, and those to the right take you to Billopp Ave. If you take the middle foot path, you will reach a "T" along the margin of the Wards Point wetland and marsh. Turn left and you will reach the beach. Turn right along the beach and walk one-third mile to **Wards Point** or an additional half mile to the **Conference House**. You can make the one-mile return trip by walking back along the beach until you see access to a street on your left. When you reach the street, turn left to reach Brighton St. Or you can take the quicker road route by following Satterlee and Surf Avenue to Billopp to Brighton Street (see map).

How You Can Help:
Housing development threatens to destroy the **southernmost pond and wetland in NY State** (Wards Point Wetland). The wetlands keep the coastal waters healthy for rich clam and oyster beds, commercial and recreational fishing and for aquatic birds. Plans for housing would destroy the 40-acre Willow Oak Woods at the east end of Conference House Park, where rare pawpaw trees, endangered willow oak, and hybrid oaks live. Please write to Gov. George Pataki (Exec. Chamber, Albany, NY 12224); request him to purchase the Pawpaw wetland and add it to Conference House Park.

For information on nature walks or special events, or to join efforts to protect the park, contact:
- Conference House Association, Box 171, SI, NY 10307, 984-6046
- Conference House-Raritan Bay Conservancy   see
- Protectors of Pine Oak Woods   addresses
- NY City Dept. of Parks and Recreation   in Appendix

Conference House

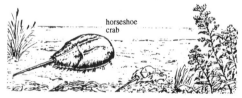

horseshoe
crab

KINGFISHER AND WOOD DUCK PONDS: BACKYARD BEAUTY .... FLOOD PROTECTION, ALL IN ONE

Marvel at the largest concentration of ducks on the island. If you're lucky, you may see the wood duck, our most colorful bird (eight colors -- count 'em!). You might also see the raucous acrobatic kingfisher. Enjoy the serenity of gentle walks through shady woods, hidden only a stone's throw from people's doorsteps. Oh yes, don't miss those phantom streets and disappearing walls!

Distance: 0.8 mile each for Kingfisher Pond and Wood Duck Pond
Level of Difficulty: easy
Things to Bring: a love of watching wildlife; binoculars, bird book, plastic bags to pick up litter, bug protection. Know your poison ivy (occasional here).

Scenic Delights:
Kingfisher Pond Staten Island's spanking new Bluebelt park was just purchased from developers only months before this book was published. Even its trail blazes are barely dry. However, the 23-acre parcel has been doing full service for the community ... well ... forever: free flood protection and water pollution treatment, outdoor recreation and neighborhood beauty, literally out the doorsteps of hundreds of homes. What more could you ask!
Wildlife at Your Doorstep The eight-acre lake is a favorite fishing area for kingfishers, egrets -- and people. The pond was named after its star acrobat, the kingfisher, whose profile is outlined on the metal gate at the entrance trail. The kingfisher looks like a stocky, scruffy-headed blue jay. It is called the "king of fishers" because of its spectacular head-first dives into the water. It steals the show even from its larger fishing relatives, the herons, and gulls. Don't expect to see the kingfisher during any single visit. It comes and goes when it wants, like any wild creature. Patience, sharp eyes and binoculars are needed. Other stunning birds you might see are glossy ibis, graceful herons, the great egret, and the most exquisitely graceful one of all, the snowy egret. On the pond, look for turtles and frogs, and listen to the chorus of spring peepers in March or April.

kingfisher

Wood Duck Pond Only yards from the bustle of Amboy Road, this secret beauty spot lies tucked away in the heart of the Great Kills neighborhood. The four-acre pond also plays a

The wood duck is our most decorated and colorful bird.

critical flood and pollution prevention role. However, its distinction is its wildlife spectacle -- for those who make sure to look for it.

"Wall-to-Wall Ducks" -- that's how Wood Duck Pond has been described at the peak of the duck migration. In April and October, as many as 150 ducks at one time have been seen here! This is one of the greatest concentrations anywhere in NY City.

The pond was named after the wood duck because it also has the greatest concentration of this uncommon and very shy bird. The wood duck is known as the most beautiful duck and the most colorful northeastern bird (eight colors). As with Kingfisher Pond, it also has gobs of other wildlife: egrets, herons, large snapping turtles, woodpeckers, song birds. It is also home to the rare eyed-brown butterfly, until now, thought to have been exterminated from Staten Island. It survives here because a rare plant community exists here, one of the only such habitats in NY City -- the tussock sedge swamp.

Phantom Streets and Disappearing Stone Walls Two curious features need some explanation. Both Kingfisher and Wood Duck Ponds and their surrounding woods are missing from official road maps. Instead, the maps all show ten square blocks of *non-existent* streets crisscrossing where these ponds and green spaces *actually exist*. Why? Because city planners and developers decades ago planned to "build out" onto every possible square block, without regard to whether there are lakes or flooding or potential park land! The streets became the "reality on paper." It is only because caring and committed citizens fought to set aside these precious lands that urban sprawl on Staten Island didn't eliminate its scenic areas.

In Kingfisher Pond Park, old stone walls -- five blocks long! -- cross through the forest and disappear into the water. They originated when colonial settlers, probably in the 1700s, built them while clearing the land for farming. When built, they stood neat and upright. Today, they are collapsed rows of boulders, no longer piled and fitted into each other. Two to three centuries of frost heaves, soil erosion, settling and human disturbance have made them look as they do today. As you walk over these walls, stop and imagine a Dutch colonial meadow surrounding you.

The walls also descend into the pond and extend along its bottom. You can see them as stepping stones crossing the south end of the pond. Apparently, as the area was built up around it, more water was directed into the pond (remember its flood prevention role?), enlarging its shoreline and submerging the walls.

How to Get To Kingfisher Pond Park:

By S.I. Rapid Transit: Get off at Great Kills Station. Walk 3/4 mile north on Giffords Lane (or take the S54 bus) to Elkhart Street.

By Bus: Take the S54 bus to Elkhart Street off Giffords Lane, or take the S74 bus to Giffords Lane and walk two blocks to Elkhart Street.

From Giffords Lane and Elkhart, walk down Elkhart to Greaves and turn right. Walk one block to corner of Greaves and Fairfield Streets.

By Car: Take Arthur Kill Road, turn onto Giffords Lane, go two blocks to Elkhart, make a left and drive to Greaves, make a right, go to corner of Greaves and Fairfield Streets, behind P.S. 32 Annex.

At the Greaves-Fairfield corner, locate the green metal entrance gate with the kingfisher profile. Walk through the gate into the field. Fifteen feet down the trail, take the right-hand fork (is it stainless steel, or just a plastic fork?). It quickly takes you to **Kingfisher Pond**'s north shore at a clearing -- a perfect lunch, fishing and wildlife watching spot. Use binoculars to sight sunning turtles on logs. Make sure to remove others' trash when you leave!

Continue on the Blue Trail which parallels the shore, passing large rocks in the pond. The Trail curves left and crosses a field. A patch of thorny blackberry on the left is a favorite nesting place for birds. After looping around a small ravine, the trail reaches a stone wall. Patiently watch for wildlife; this is a good place to see egrets, herons and ducks, maybe even a kingfisher. In summer, it may be covered with lime-green duckweed, a minute aquatic wildflower, not "scum" or "slime." Look across the bay at the stepping stone-like series of rocks -- an ancient submerged stone wall. A footbridge may

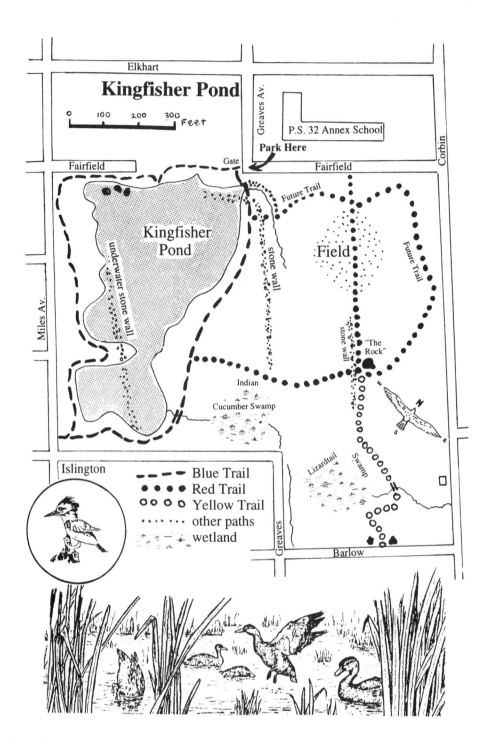

Kingfisher Pond

0   100   200   300 Feet

Elkhart

Greaves Av.

P.S. 32 Annex School

Park Here

Fairfield

Gate

Fairfield

Corbin

Kingfisher
Pond

underwater stone wall

stone wall

Future Trail

Field

Future Trail

Miles Av.

stone wall

"The Rock"

Indian
Cucumber Swamp

N

S   E

Islington

- - - - Blue Trail
● ● ● ● Red Trail
○ ○ ○ ○ Yellow Trail
· · · · · · other paths
wetland

Lizardtail   Swamp

Greaves

Barlow

Ancient stone wall submerges into Kingfisher Pond like stepping stones

be built across the narrow point in the future.

The Blue Trail next passes an access to Miles Avenue and a large willow tree. It follows along the south shore of the pond, and dips across a foot bridge over a small stream. This stream is the pond's water source. It comes from a storm water stilling pond upstream, which removes sediment ("mud").

swamp mallow

You pass through cool woods of oak, hickory, red maple, sweet gum and sassafras. Wildflowers to watch for: showy pink swamp mallow along the water edge; pinxter azalea, in the woods in spring; pink lady's slipper (illegal to pick!); and the city's largest cucumber-root colony.

Moments later, the Blue Trail meets the Red Trail. Turn right on the Red Trail. It crosses a centuries-old collapsed stone wall (and an underground stream!) Imagine that you are standing in a field as a Dutch farmer labors, dragging and placing every rock into place.

On your right, you pass by fern-filled Lizardtail Swamp. Cross another stone wall where you reach a huge boulder (placed here by the Ice Age glacier, not the farmer!). The Red Trail turns left. (The Yellow Trail to the right takes you 700 feet to Barlow Ave.)

The Red Trail parallels the stone wall and enters a grassy field. As you walk, look on your left for a large oak tree that appears to be standing on legs. It really *is* "on its last legs" -- its base was hollowed out by a fire yet it still clings to life. The trail goes over the crest of a hill. If the Red Trail extension is not yet built, the trail will end at Fairfield Street -- turn left to return to where you started. If the trail extension has been completed, it turns left before Fairfield Street. It passes the largest tree in the park, crosses a drainageway, another stone wall, and finally meets the Blue Trail.

Turn right at the Blue Trail. Cross the stone wall again, and before you jump a drainageway, notice how the wall submerges into the pond. Cross another old wall, enter a clearing Turn right exit.

How to Get to Wood Duck Pond:

By Rapid Transit: Exit at Great Kills Station. Walk south on Giffords Lane to Amboy Road. Turn right and follow Amboy through the charming village of Great Kills to Lindenwood Road. Turn Left onto Lindenwood and follow it diagonally right past P.S. 8 to Oakdale Street; turn right and walk four blocks to Ramblewood Ave. Turn right onto Ramblewood.

By Bus: Take the S79 to Amboy Road and Richmond Avenue. Walk south on Richmond Avenue one block to Oakdale Street Turn left, go ten blocks to Ramblewood, turn left, walk to its end.

By Car: Take Hylan Blvd. to Richmond Avenue. Turn north. Go five or so blocks to Oakdale (one block before Amboy Road), turn right on Oakdale, go ten blocks to Ramblewood, turn left and park on your right.

From Ramblewood, look for a path into the woods on the right. Walk *very quietly* if you want to see wood ducks. Moments later, you are at **Wood Duck Pond**. Use your binoculars to scan the water for birds. You are most likely to see "wall-to-wall ducks" if you arrive during migration season -- and with lucky timing.

Notice how this pond is hemmed in by houses. If they'd built houses over a filled-in pond, as intended, where would all the waters go during storms? ... into basements and streets!

When you finish, return to the road and turn right. Very nearby is a large wooden post on the left with a sign "Wood Duck Pond Bluebelt." Just after it, turn left into the woods. Notice how deeply shady and mature these woods are, with large beech and oaks. Look for fragrant spicebush and pinxter azalea, as well as flowering dogwood and jack-in-the-pulpit.

About 300 feet along the path, take the first left. It loops through attractive forest and returns to the first path, where you turn left. Take the next righthand path, cross a plank bridge and turn left. Pass a junked car. The path soon dead-ends at the rare **tussock sedge swamp** where the threatened eyed-brown butterfly lives. You are only yards from Amboy Road, but totally hidden.

Take the path back, but instead of crossing the plank bridge, continue straight along the stream back to Ramblewood.

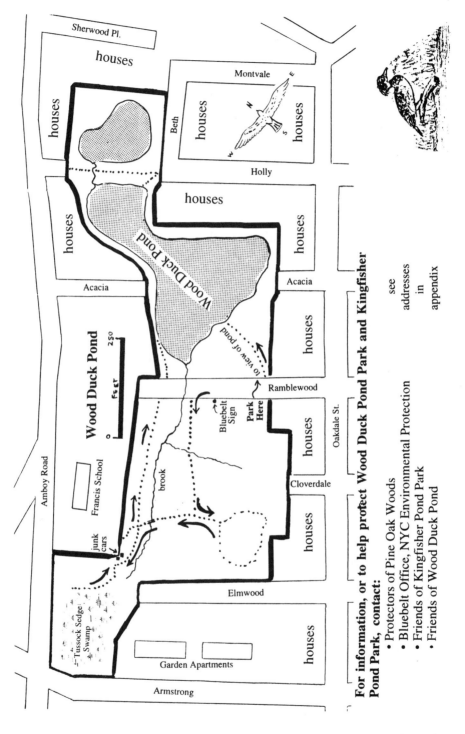

Wood Duck Pond

Feet
0   250

houses

Sherwood Pl.

houses

Montvale

Beth

houses

N
W   E
S

houses

Holly

houses

houses

Acacia

houses

Wood Duck Pond

Acacia

houses

to view of pond

Ramblewood

Oakdale St.

Bluebelt Sign

Park Here

Amboy Road

Francis School

brook

houses

Cloverdale

junk cars

houses

Tussock Sedge Swamp

Elmwood

Garden Apartments

houses

Armstrong

For information, or to help protect Wood Duck Pond Park and Kingfisher Pond Park, contact:

• Protectors of Pine Oak Woods
• Bluebelt Office, NYC Environmental Protection
• Friends of Kingfisher Pond Park
• Friends of Wood Duck Pond

see addresses in appendix

The Bluebelt: Brilliant Program Saves
Tax Dollars & Greenspace

Staten Island is unique as the only borough with both a Greenbelt and a Bluebelt. The Bluebelt is a brilliant program to purchase wetlands to prevent their destruction from development. Why should tax dollars be used to buy "swamps" (and streams and ponds)? Because using Nature's storm sewers -- swamps, streams and ponds -- save millions of dollars, both tax dollars and personal expenses, and enhance the tax base. Here's why: **Swamps, wetlands and ponds retain flood waters and release them slowly, preventing flooding.** This is how they save both money *and* the environment:

- prevents or reduces flooding after major storms .... and the property damage flooding causes
- saves the costs of installing or enlarging expensive storm sewers
- filters street runoff and pollution which
  - reduces the need for tax dollars to operate water pollution programs
  - keeps lake, bay and ocean waters cleaner, which fosters a thriving beach, fishing, boating and tourism industry. Polluted waters damage and discourage recreational, income-producing assets.
- greenspace, ponds and park land enhance home property values by maintaining neighborhood beauty, and giving a selling advantage to those who live near. Homes near a park usually command higher prices than similar homes not near one.
- improves quality of life for neighborhoods by providing outdoor recreation, enjoyment in seeing wildlife and greenery, and reducing neighborhood crowding and congestion (by occupying land in a beneficial way that would otherwise be densely filled in with shoulder-to-shoulder subdivisions).

The Bluebelt has created greenspace corridors and added many parks (some of which are described in this book), including Blue Heron Park (the first), Long Pond Park, Lemon Creek, Jacks Pond, Kingfisher Pond Park, and Wood Duck Pond, to name a few.

The Sweetbrook Watershed in particular (which includes Wood Duck Pond) is notorious for severe neighborhood flooding. This was caused by uncaring planning by past developers and city planning officials. All taxpayers have had to pay for the damage and expenses in these flood-prone areas. While the citizen campaign to purchase Wood Duck Pond was underway in the early 1990s, one resident wrote a letter to a city councilman describing what happened on Holly Avenue adjacent to the pond: "When pilings were driven into the ground [to build a row of houses], the water in the Wood Duck Pond rose and the last house next to the pond tipped." The letter adds, "another example of poor planning was the building of an apartment complex on Armstrong and Leverett Avenues where unsuspecting new tenant owners found their cars floating and ending up on top of one another in a parking lot after a severe rainstorm."

BLUE HERON PARK: A TRANQUIL SANCTUARY TO RENEW YOURSELF

A perfect place to "commune with nature." Stroll around tranquil ponds, rich with water lilies and wildlife, including the park's namesake, the magnificent great blue heron. Colorful wildflowers dot the ponds and peaceful forest. Enjoy a guided tour. Don't forget to admire the Great Old Oak, a Colonial-era survivor.

Distance: 1.8 mile loop
Level of Difficulty: easy
Things to Bring: bug and tick protection, binoculars, camera, bird and flower guides. Know your poison ivy (occasional here).

Scenic Delights:

Tranquil Ponds With trails winding past tranquil and elegant ponds, this is an ideal place to "commune with nature." Blue Heron Park protects six peaceful ponds filled with wildlife and waterlilies. The pond basins (called glacial kettleholes) were sculpted out by the Ice Age glacier. The largest ponds are 1.75-acre Spring Pond, covered with exquisite white water lilies, and 1.4-acre Blue Heron Pond, covered with swamp loosestrife. The clean ponds have been described as "clear water in a natural bowl."

Credit: James Rossi

Haven for Wildlife This is the place to stroll quietly, not just to maintain the meditative atmosphere of this place, but so that the birds won't fly off before your arrival! If you remain quiet, the great blue heron, our tallest bird, can be seen along the ponds. You can admire this four-foot high stork-like bird along with others such as the 38-inch high great egret, the curve-billed glossy ibis (recently arrived from the tropics), and the exquisite black-crowned night heron.

If you're really lucky (and quiet), you may also get

Graceful great blue heron, our state's tallest bird

Credit: Mike Feller, c 1998

Tranquillity awaits you at lily-padded Spring Pond, Blue Heron Park

to see the shy wood duck (with eight colors, our most decorated bird) and the elusive osprey (large eagle relative). Watch for kingfisher, muskrat and raccoon. Three kinds of owls and other birds can be sighted.

Also watch for painted and snapping turtles sunning on logs in the ponds. The woods contain protected box and wood turtles (illegal to collect!). Spring peepers and other frogs break the smooth dark surface of Spring Pond.

Colorful and Rare Wildflowers Cheerful wildflower displays add to the elegance of Blue Heron Park. White water lilies, the scarlet cardinal flower (along pond margins), two kinds of orchids, the seductively scented pinxter azalea, the blaze-orange butterflyweed -- these are just a few of the bright (and illegal to pick) wildflowers.

cardinal flower

The Great Old Oak On the bank of Blue Heron Brook, reached by the Towering Trees Trail, is a great old oak, six feet in diameter and probably at least 250 years old. Admire the stately tulip trees and large black oaks along this trail.

Outdoor Programs The park has just erected an attractive visitor and environmental education center that offers free guided tours, school and youth nature programs, arts, crafts and photography workshops. You can also enjoy fall concerts, fishing, picnicking and a trail for the handicapped.

How to Get There:

By S.I. Rapid Transit: Exit at Annadale Station. Walk south on Annadale Road to Poillon Avenue. Follow Poillon a half mile to the park entrance.

By Bus: Take S78 or S59 to Poillon Ave. Walk north 0.5 mi. to entrance.

By Car: Via West Shore Expressway and Richmond Parkway, exit at Arden Avenue. Take Arden south to Hylan, turn right, drive 0.6 mile to Poillon Avenue. Turn right, go half mile to park entrance. Via Hylan Blvd., take it south of Great Kills. Poillon Avenue is slightly more than one mile past Hylan's junction with Richmond Avenue.

From the parking lot, stop in the Visitor Center and check out the programs. From the Visitor Center, head toward the large wooden shelter. The Spring Pond Trail loop begins to the **right** of the shelter. The trail winds through a quiet forest of sweet gum, red maple, sour gum and ash trees. **Avoid trail-side poison ivy.** Soon, **Spring Pond** appears in view. Have your binoculars ready and walk quietly if you want to see those herons before they take off. If you get to see a **blue heron**, admire its graceful form in the water and its agile thrust for fish. If one flies up, note how gawky it looks and how it reminds you of a pterodactyl, the flying dinosaur. (You mean you haven't seen a pterodactyl lately?) Use the bird blind (wooden viewing windows) for fool-proof wildlife watching. Don't miss the **white flowers of the water lily**.

Continue on the Spring Pond Trail to the other end of the pond. The woods have now changed to oak and sassafras. Just before Poillon Avenue (pronounced "poo-yon"), the trail turns left over a new walkway across the end of Spring Pond. A 100 feet later is a fork in the trail (don't look for silverware, silly!). The left fork is the

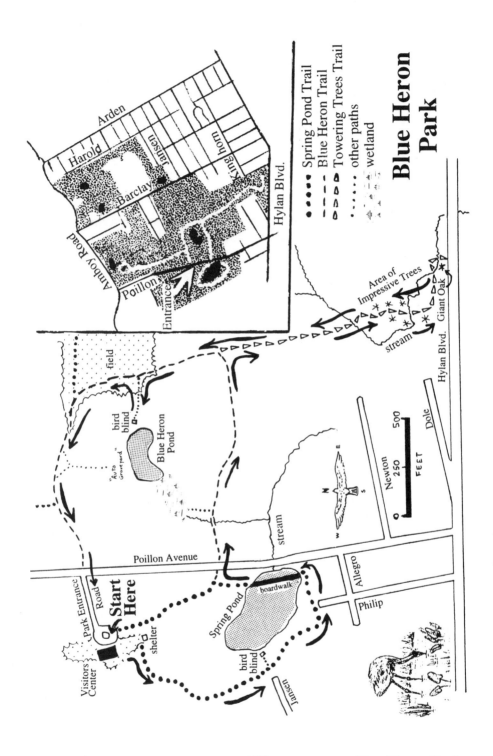

Blue Heron Park

Spring Pond Trail
Blue Heron Trail
Towering Trees Trail
other paths
wetland

Area of Impressive Trees

Giant Oak

stream

Hylan Blvd.

field

bird blind

"Auto Graveyard"

Blue Heron Pond

stream

Newton

Dole

FEET

0   250   500

Poillon Avenue

Allegro

Philip

Start Here

Park Entrance Road

Visitors Center

shelter

Spring Pond

boardwalk

bird blind

Jansen

Arden

Harold

Jansen

Barclay

Kinghorn

Amboy Road

Poillon

Entrance

Hylan Blvd.

handicap trail back to the Visitor Center. Make a right on the Blue Heron Trail, which crosses the road and into the east section.

In the woods again, cross a wooden foot bridge. A small side foot path dead-ends in 200 feet at a wetland used by groups to sample wetland creatures. In 800 feet, the trail comes to a "T." Turn right on the Towering Trees Trail (green-blazed). Notice how the woods quickly become mature, with large, stately trunks of tulip trees, oaks and beech. The deep woods at the winding, babbling brook look like a scene right out of the Catskills, not NY City! Appreciate the high red banks cut by the brook.

Cross the brook and follow the green blazes of the trail until it descends to another wide bend of the brook. At this bend, notice a very large tree 15 feet from the brook. This is the **Great Old Oak**. Observe its swollen, knobby trunk on your right. This venerable survivor has been around through most of Staten Island's European history. Walk up to the tree and put your hand on it to really appreciate its size (you can even hug it!).

You may notice the sound of traffic. Hard to believe, but Hylan Blvd. is up the steep slope only 100 feet away! However, it's not time to re-enter civilization -- take the same trail back again. When you return to the trail intersection with the Blue Heron Trail, continue straight.

A hundred feet later, watch on your left when the woods end and a clearing appears. Turn down this left-hand path to an observation platform overlooking **Blue Heron Pond**. Walk quietly or you may scare the herons, wood duck or other shy birds.

Return to the Blue Heron Trail and turn left. It follows the margin of a thicket and then re-enters the woods. The first side path on your left leads to a valley named the "Auto Graveyard" because 30 stolen, junked cars were hauled out several years ago! In about 100 feet, you can also explore another side trail on your right, the blue-blazed North Woodlands Trail (use the map). When the Blue Heron Trail reaches the road, look for the parking lot across the street.

Credit: Harry Madden

For information or to help protect the park, contact (addresses in appendix):
- Friends of Blue Heron Park
- Protectors of Pine Oak Woods
- Blue Heron Park Visitor Center

Snowy egret, exquisite in plumage display

EXPLORING LONG POND THROUGH A MAZE OF TRAILS

Weave through a maze of trails past pretty ponds and impressive trees. Discover a park so new, its painted trail blazes are barely dry. It may be new, but it preserves an old landscape -- rural southern Staten Island as if frozen in time. It is also the southernmost landscape created by the Ice Age glaciers, east of the Mississippi. Visit picturesque Long Pond, a secluded reserve for wildlife and rare plants.

Distance: 1.8 mile round trip

Level of Difficulty: easy

Things to Bring: Camera, binoculars, bird guide, bug repellent, compass, plastic bags to pick up litter, fishing gear. Know your poison ivy (occasional to common here).

Scenic Delights:
Long Pond Reminding one of a scene out of the Catskills, five-acre Long Pond is largely unknown to Staten Islanders or anybody else. It is unusual because, at 65 feet above sea level, it has no incoming streams, even though it is only 3/4 mile from the sea. Long Pond is the largest of the preserve's seven ponds, all created when the Ice Age glacier molded the landscape into little knobs and kettleholes 15,000 years ago. It is the _southernmost landscape (called "knob and kettle") east of the Mississippi that was molded by the continental glaciers_ . Those ponds and other pockets of wetland are one of the newest additions to Staten Island's park system (it won't be officially dedicated until 1999). They include the Page Avenue Bluebelt, preserving an adjacent pond system which in turn protects human communities from flooding (and waste of tax dollars -- see page 134).
Rural Staten Island, Frozen in Time Long Pond Park preserves southern Staten Island as it looked before the housing boom and urban sprawl. More than 300 years of European settlement of Staten Island has not changed the rural character of Long Pond, one of the least populated areas of New York City. Long Pond abuts the 19th century pastoral landscape of Mt. Loretto (see page 114). Together, they feature 110 acres of Staten Island's irreplaceable pre-urban landscape. Its scenic and ecological importance was recognized in 1975 by the City Planning Commission and its wetlands were given some protection in the mid-1980s. But this

Long Pond

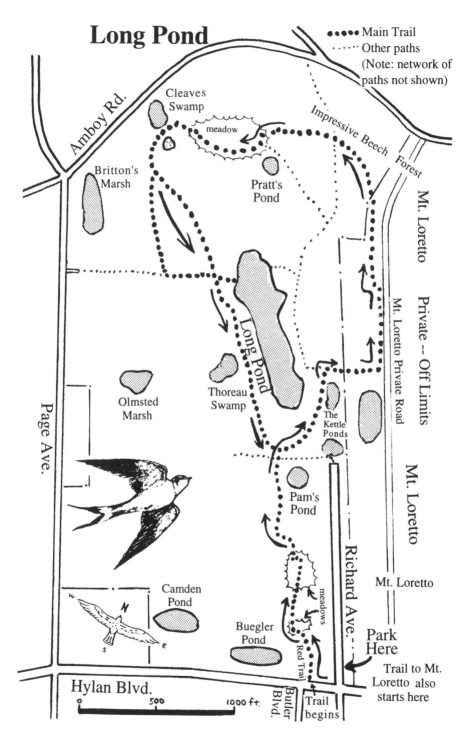

Main Trail
Other paths
(Note: network of paths not shown)

Amboy Rd.

Cleaves Swamp

meadow

Impressive Beech Forest

Britton's Marsh

Pratt's Pond

Mt. Loretto   Private -- Off Limits

Mt. Loretto Private Road

Long Pond

Olmsted Marsh

Thoreau Swamp

The Kettle Ponds

Page Ave.

Pam's Pond

Mt. Loretto

Camden Pond

W   N   E   S

Buegler Pond

Richard Ave.

Red Trail

meadows

Park Here

Trail to Mt. Loretto also starts here

Hylan Blvd.

0   500   1000 ft.

Butler Blvd.

Trail begins

didn't stop an attempt to turn the site into housing development in 1988. An environmental struggle ensued, led by Protectors of Pine Oak Woods. Now Long Pond Park is saved and open to the public.

How to Get There:

By Bus: Take the S78 down Hylan Blvd., just past the entrance to Mt. Loretto, to Richard Avenue.

By Car: Take S.I. Expressway west to the West Shore Expressway (Rte. 440 South). Take it almost to the end, following signs to "Outerbridge Exit." As you approach the Outerbridge, take the last exit before the toll. Do not continue onto the Outerbridge or you will be forced into New Jersey! The exit puts you onto Veterans Road West. Turn left off Veterans onto an overpass, then make a right onto Boscombe Avenue. At the end of Boscombe, turn left onto Page Avenue. Take Page Avenue south to Hylan Blvd. Make a left on Hylan, drive to the first street on the left, Richard Avenue. Park on Richard Avenue near Hylan.

Suggestion: This is also the place to begin your walk to the dramatic bluffs of Mt. Loretto. Why not consider doing both on the same day!

Standing on Richard Avenue *(on the forested side of Hylan),* turn right onto Hylan. Walk only 200 feet to the second telephone pole (it has the sign "Butler Blvd."). Turn right onto the trail.

Watch for poison ivy along the trail. When the trail comes to a meadow, with a view into someone's backyard, bear left and back onto the woods trail.

Instead of exhausting the reader with repeated directions of "turn left," "turn right," and "go straight," the rule here is "**Always follow the red trail blazes!**" This is an incredible maze of foot paths -- in the first mile, there are more than 30 trail forks and junctions!

When the Red Trail enters a second meadow, dense with tall wildflowers, continue straight (not right). In a few minutes, enter an attractive rust-colored sand barrens with little birch and aspen trees. Be careful near the prickly brier. At the third clearing is a four-way junction; turn right. The woods are now oak and sassafras. Soon, you reach duckweed-covered **Pam's Pond**, where you can see herons, egrets and wood duck if you are quiet. Skirt the pond on the left.

Shortly after, the Red Trail forks. You take the *right fork*. In 500 feet, you pass one of the partly hidden **Kettle Ponds** on the right. The Red Trail now turns right. Moments later, you are on the private property of Mt. Loretto institution. When you reach the private drive, turn left, following red blazes. **Do not take any other paths -- they are off-limits.**

The Red Trail veers to the left away from the road. In a few minutes, it re-enters the park. The forest is now **impressive beech** and oak trees, some more than 150 years old! Some of the beech are among the largest in the city. It is unclear why the earlier owners never cut it down. Note when you leave the mature forest and suddenly enter the much younger woods. This was probably a meadow only 75 years ago. Moments later, enter a large meadow. Bear left along the meadow and re-enter the woods on the Red Trail.

About six trail forks later, you dip into a little ravine, passing your third junked car (an eyesore that will hopefully be removed by park staff -- remember, this *just* became a protected park). After the ravine, take the next right. This is a temporary route to avoid water holes created in the trail by heavy vehicles while removing junked stolen cars. (If this trail route is changed in the future, just remember, *"Always follow the Red Trail!"*) The woods road comes to a wide junction. Construction vehicles created this while hauling out the cars. Ignore the litter, which has yet to be removed.

Turn left at this junction. In a few minutes, you arrive at **Long Pond**, at a fishing spot used by neighborhood kids. Remind yourself that you are still in New York City! Look for the pink flowers of the swamp rose mallow dotting the shore in July or August. Scan the opposite shore for herons or ducks. Do your part to return this formerly neglected area to its fullest beauty by picking up some of the litter.

swamp mallow

Continue down the Red Trail, passing approximately five trail forks (but don't pass any spoons or knives!). You have now returned to Pam's Pond, which you last saw 28 trail forks ago!

Return on the Red Trail, passing the earlier three meadows and you end up on Hylan Blvd.

How You Can Help:

To the south of Long Pond Park, across Hylan Blvd. just beyond Page Avenue, is a 40-acre wooded wetland on the Atlantic Migratory Bird Flyway that is about to be destroyed for housing. The Willow Oak Woods contain many rare plants, including a rare colony of pawpaw trees (which yield a tasty fruit), as well as rare oak hybrids. The wetlands also keep adjacent coastal waters healthy for rich clam and oyster beds, commercial and recreational fishing and for waterfowl. Please write to the Governor (Exec. Chamber, Albany, NY 12224) and request him to have the state purchase the Willow Oak Woods and add it to Conference House Park.

For information or to support protection efforts, contact:
- Protectors of Pine Oak Woods   see addresses
- NY City Dept. of Parks and Recreation   in appendix
- Community Board 3, 655 Rossville Av. SI 10309 356-7900

Secluded Long Pond, a favorite fishing spot for birds ... and kids!

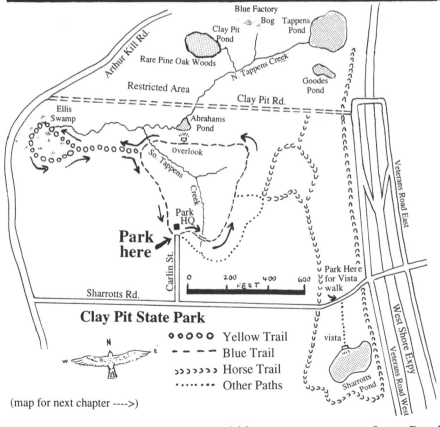

Blue Factory

Bog
Tappens
Pond

Clay Pit
Pond

Arthur Kill Rd.

Rare Pine Oak Woods

N. Tappens Creek

Goodes
Pond

Restricted Area

Clay Pit Rd.

Ellis
Swamp

Abrahams
Pond

Overlook

So. Tappens Creek

Park
HQ

**Park
here**

Carlin St.

0   200   400   600
FEET

Park Here
for Vista
walk

Veterans Road East

West Shore Expy

Veterans Road West

vista

Sharrotts Rd.

Sharrotts
Pond

Clay Pit State Park

N
W   E
S

○○○○○ Yellow Trail
‒ ‒ ‒ ‒ Blue Trail
＞＞＞＞＞ Horse Trail
• • • • • • • Other Paths

(map for next chapter ---->)

CLAY PIT PARK: A PIECE OF
THE SOUTH SURVIVES

Visit the "Sandy Ground," New York City's only pine-oak barrens landscape. It is home to unique trees and wildlife typical of the South.

Distance: 1.5 mile round trip

Level of Difficulty: easy

Things to Bring: Bug protection, camera, binoculars, tree and flower guides. Know your poison ivy (occasional to common here).

Scenic Delights:

Clay Pit Pond Preserve "A cool and pleasant retreat, but a hungry soil." These are the words of the famous naturalist Henry David Thoreau, as he described the infertile sandy grounds of southern Staten Island in 1843.

Today, the 260-acre Clay Pit Pond State Park Preserve still harbors these sandy pine-oak woods, the only place in New York City where it survives. Its landscape is typical of the South. It is indeed one of the northernmost places where several southern animals and plants live, such as the fence lizard (introduced in 1946 by a zoo official), Virginia pine and blackjack oak. Rare wildflowers include cranberry, lizard-tail, possum-haw and bog twayblade.

blackjack oak

The "pine-oak woods" of this park is also "preserved" in the name of Staten Island's foremost environmental organization, Protectors of Pine Oak Woods. It is no coincidence, for the organization named itself after this site when the group formed to save these woods and ponds from destruction in 1972. It is also New York City's only state park preserve.

As is true for most of Staten Island's natural parks, it required an intense citizen campaign to save Clay Pit Ponds from the bulldozer. This campaign led to the creation of Protectors of Pine Oak Woods. It had a predecessor, however, the S.I. Greenbelt Natural Areas League (SIGNAL). This group, formed in 1964, succeeded in blocking the two highway projects which would have destroyed the Greenbelt.

The Preserve's most unique area, the pine and oak sand barrens and ponds, is very sensitive to human impact. Therefore, it is currently off limits to the public and walking is permitted only on two short nature trails near the park headquarters. Access is only allowed with a special research permit.

The 130 million year-old clay mined in the area yielded outstanding fossils of dawn redwoods, amber, maple, tortoises and even animal bones. Samples are now housed in the S.I. Institute.

How to Get There

By Bus: From the S.I. Ferry, take the S74 bus to Sharrotts Road. Walk across Arthur Kill Road to Sharrotts Road, then walk down Sharrotts Road one-quarter mile to Carlin Street. Turn left onto Carlin, follow it one block to the end.

By Car: Take the S.I. Expressway to the West Shore Expressway (Rte. 440 South). Drive five miles on West Shore to Exit 3 (Bloomingdale Road). At the end of the exit ramp, turn left on Bloomingdale Road, then make a right on Sharrotts Road. Cross over the West Shore Exp'y. (If you want to take a short detour to a pretty pond, immediately park after crossing the Exp'y. Look on your left for a foot trail that takes you 300 feet to an overlook over Sharrotts Pond.) Continue on Sharrotts Avenue to Carlin Street. Turn right on Carlin and drive to its end.

There are two foot trails, the Abraham's Pond Trail (blue blazes) and the Ellis Swamp Trail (yellow).

Walk behind the Park headquarters building to the picnic area behind it. The Abraham's Pond Trail begins to the right of the picnic area. This trail takes you past beehives, a woodshed, and across a steep ravine through woods and a field. It then enters a large dry, open sandy area with stunted trees. This is the edge of the rare **sand barrens** community that makes the preserve unique in New York City. The rare fence lizard and desert-like prickly pear cactus live here.

After awhile, the trail reaches an observation platform over **Abraham's Pond**. It is named after Abraham Ellis who did clay mining here in the 1800s. The pond is actually a former clay mining pit from the 1800s and Nature gradually transformed it into this beautiful marsh, filled with wildlife.

prickly pear cactus

A few minutes after leaving the pond, the Blue Trail arrives at the Yellow Trail. Turn right and you will pass by a natural spring and a swamp which displays the bizarre skunk cabbage. Your route again passes through sandy, scrubby woods with thorny catbrier and aromatic sassafras. The trail crosses Ellis Swamp along boardwalks. It ultimately loops back to the Blue Trail. Turn right at the Blue Trail and you return to the Park Headquarters. Be sure to admire the Wildflower Garden on the side of the park building.

skunk cabbage

The park offers guided tours and other fascinating programs. Check the schedule of events at the park office.

For information or to help protect the park, contact:

- Clay Pit State Park Preserve, 83 Nielsen Ave.,SI, NY, 10309 718-967-1976
- Protectors of Pine Oak Woods   see address in appendix

sassafras

Index

JOIN PROTECTORS -- HELP PROTECT STATEN ISLAND'S PARKS AND NATURAL AREAS!

Protectors of Pine Oak Woods (PPOW) is Staten Island's primary environmental group dedicated to protecting the Island's parks, natural areas, ponds and wildlife. Since 1972, Protectors has been the instrumental citizen force that helped save thousands of acres of parks and preserves from destruction. These beautiful places are now open for everybody -- people and wildlife -- to use and enjoy.

Protectors also sponsors dozens of walks a year in the Greenbelt and other natural areas. Our newsletter informs members of threats to the environment. We award annual scholarships to students to attend the State's Ecology Camp in upstate NY, and also present environmental awards at school science fairs.

Our 2500 members are proud that we at Protectors:
• were instrumental in establishing the 3000-acre Greenbelt, one of the country's largest urban parks
• successfully advocated establishment of NY City's only State Park Preserve at Clay Pit Ponds
• successfully lobbied for adoption of the Bluebelt, which created natural flood protection zones (protecting property and saving millions in taxpayer money) and also created many neighborhood parks
• helped establish numerous parks such as Blue Heron, Kingfisher Pond, Wood Duck Pond, Long Pond and Arbutus Woods
• successfully fought to save Willowbrook's Corson Brook Woods and its ancient trees and rare plants from destruction
• successfully lobbied the state to purchase Camp Kaufman, with easements that allow its continued use as a camp
• were responsible in 1998 for saving the Island's secret jewel, St. Francis Seminary Woodlands which was added to the Greenbelt
• currently working to assure that the magnificent Mt. Loretto-by-the-Sea, Willow Oak Woods and other sites are permanently protected

---

PROTECTORS OF PINE OAK WOODS

STATEN ISLAND'S LAND CONSERVATION ORGANIZATION

clip and mail

YES, I want to be a Partner in helping to save Staten Island's natural treasures & Greenbelt !

Please enroll me as a member in the following category:

_____ $ 5.00...Student
_____ $ 5.00...Senior Citizen
_____ $ 10.00...Individual
_____ $ 15.00...Family
_____ $ 25.00...Organizational
_____ $ 25.00...Contributing (includes free lapel pin)
_____ $ 50.00...Patron (includes 2 lapel pins)
_____ $100.00...Donor (includes 2 lapel pins)
_____ $100.00 & Up...Corporate (includes 2 lapel pins)
_____ $ 3.50...Lapel Pin, mailed to me

Membership is Tax Deductible

MAIL TO:
Sylvia Zaage
160 Simonson Ave.
Staten Island, NY
10303

NAME   (Mr. Mrs. Ms.) _____

ADDRESS_____ ZIP _____

TELEPHONE (   )_____ ☐ Phone me. I want to volunteer my help

ENCLOSED is my tax deductible check for $_____ Make payable to Protectors of Pine Oak Woods, Inc.

ADDRESSES

Bluebelt Office, NYC Dept. of Environmental Protection 59-17 Junction Blvd. Elmhurst, Ny 11368

Coalition for Amundsen Trailway, 85 Clarke Ave. S.I., NY 10306

Conference House-Raritan Bay Conservancy 263 Manhattan St., SI, NY 10307   718-356-6368

Friends of Blue Heron Park c/o Jack Baird 48 Poillon Av. S.I., NY 10312 718 317-1732

S.I. **Friends of Clearwater** , PO Box 270, S.I., NY 10305 718-273-9093

Friends of Kingfisher Pond Park, c/o Pichler, 137 Islington St., S.I. 10308 967-9362

Friends of Wood Duck Pond, c/o Bianco, 150 Ramblewood Av., S.I. 10308

Gateway Nat'l Recreation Area, S.I. Unit, Miller Field, S.I., NY 10306, 351-6970

S.I. **Greenbelt Park** Office 200 Nevada Ave., S.I., NY 10306   667-2165

Greenbelt Conservancy 200 Nevada Ave., S.I., NY 10306   718-667-2165

Jacques Marchais **Museum of Tibetan Art**, 340 Lighthouse Ave., SI. 10306, 987-3500

Mariners Marsh Conservancy, c/o Howard Snyder Box 40764, S.I., NY 10304

Natural Resources Protective Assoc., PO Box 40270, SI, NY 10304 718-987-6037

NY City **Audubon Society**, Rm. 606, 71 W. 23rd St. NY, NY 212-691-7483

NY City Parks & Recreation The Arsenal, Central Park NewYork, NY 10021 212- 360-1331

NY City **Parks & Recreation (S.I.)** 1150 Clove Rd. SI, NY 10301 718-390-8000

NY State Dept. of Environmental Conservation 47-40 21st St., Long Is. City, NY 11101 718-482-4900

NY - NJ Trail Conference, 232 Madison Ave., Rm. 401 NY, NY 10016 212 685-9698

Office of **Borough President** Borough Hall, SI, NY 10301 718-816-2000

Protectors of Pine Oak Woods , 80 Mann Ave., S.I., NY 10314 718-761-7496

Sierra Club, NYC Chapter 2nd Floor, 625 Broadway, NewYork, NY 10012 212-473-7841

S.I. Citizens for Clean Air, c/o Helen Bialer, Pres. 47 Commerce St., S.I., NY 10314, 718-698-8160

S.I. Historical Society 441 Clarke Av., SI, NY 10306   718-351-1611

S.I. Institute of Arts & Sciences, 75 Stuyvesant Place, SI,NY 10301, 718-727-1135

S.I. Zoo, Clove Rd., SI, NY, 10310   718-442-3100

Sweetbay Magnolia Bio-Reserve Conservancy, c/o R. Lynch, 17 Monroe Ave. SI, NY 10301   273-3740

Urban Trail Club 2025 29th St., Long Island City, NY 11105-2501

Credit: Harry Madden

Autumn serenity at Ohrbach Lake in the heart of the Greenbelt